Every Step
of the Way

Every Step of the Way

Stories by Teenagers 4

Edited by
Michael Wilt

Saint Mary's Press
Christian Brothers Publications
Winona, Minnesota

Genuine recycled paper with 10% post-consumer waste. Printed with soy-based ink.

Jessica Carnicom, cover artist, Notre Dame Academy, Toledo, OH

The publishing team included Michael Wilt, development editor; Laurie A. Berg, copy editor; James H. Gurley, production editor; Maurine R. Twait, art director; Laurie Geisler, cover designer; pre-press, printing, and binding by the graphics division of Saint Mary's Press.

The quotation by William Carlos Williams on page 11 is quoted in *The Call of Stories: Teaching and the Moral Imagination*, by Robert Coles (Boston: Houghton Mifflin Company, 1989), page 30. Copyright © 1989 by Robert Coles.

The excerpt on page 104 is from *The Color Purple*, by Alice Walker (New York: Pocket Books, a division of Simon and Schuster, 1985), pages 202–203. Copyright © 1982 by Alice Walker.

Printed in the United States of America

Printing: 9 8 7 6 5 4 3 2 1

Year: 2007 06 05 04 03 02 01 00 99

ISBN 0-88489-581-5

Tracy de Escobar
Coyle-Cassidy
High School
Taunton, Maryland

Contents

Michael Wilt
Editor

Preface

Storytellers

We are all storytellers. We can hardly get through a normal day without telling a story or two, and for each one we tell, we are bound to hear one from someone else. Our stories may be simple or ordinary—something we did over the weekend. They may be profound or important—the story of a grandparent or great-grandparent we never knew. Some of our stories are just for fun—made-up jokes or stories of true events that cause laughter. Long before television started presenting hour after hour of "funniest videos," people told stories, over and over, about the wedding cake that toppled over or the toddler who covered herself with shaving cream. A thousand words, accompanied by tears of laughter, often were worth far more than pictures.

By telling stories we entertain and inform, but we also grow in self-understanding. Sometimes such growth happens simply through the telling of the story: After hearing ourselves tell our own tale, we see or understand what happened in a new light. We say "Aha!" or "Now I get it!" Sometimes we tell our story to someone else in the hope that they will help us interpret our experience from a different perspective. If we feel stuck about a particular issue or aspect of life, we are often inclined to find a good listener and talk about it with him or her. We swap stories.

Stories and Faith

Matters of faith also lend themselves to the telling of stories. This is not surprising—the sacred writings of the world's religions, after all, consist in large part of gatherings of stories about key figures of the particular faith. In Christianity the Gospels tell stories about what Jesus did and taught. Jesus himself used stories, parables, to illustrate his teachings.

The use of stories in religion doesn't stop with the Scriptures. Faith is shared from one generation to the next by word of mouth. Parents tell young children the stories of Jesus' life, death, and Resurrection, and the children's understanding of these stories grows and changes as they mature. Faith is shared among peers as well, as schoolmates tell one another the stories that best explain faith for them. Experiences of loss, gain, and doubt become the new stories that help us find our way in our journey of faith.

Every Step of the Way: Stories by Teenagers 4 is the latest volume of stories written by teenagers and published by Saint Mary's Press. For this volume we asked teenagers to submit first-person, true stories that address the question, "What has been an important experience for you of God's presence or absence?" The forty-seven stories collected here were selected from hundreds of submissions from all over the country. Many of these stories have probably never been told before—the subject matter has a highly personal nature, for God's presence (and absence) is often experienced in the course of circumstances and events that are quite private. We thank all our student writers for bravely shaking off any inhibitions and allowing us a glimpse into their lives.

In these stories we are privileged to witness great losses that lead to enrichment and faith. We witness the receiving of gifts that are so fulfilling that the recipients can imagine only one possible source, a loving God. For these writers God is present, whether in despair or in joy. We also witness pain and loss in which the writers can find no evidence of God's presence, leading them to be angry with God or to deny God's existence entirely. Throughout this collection our storytellers face challenging moments and grasp them as opportunities to learn and grow, always aware that learning is not easy and growth can be painful.

Hearing Others' Stories

For readers, these stories may strike common chords. They may call to mind similar experiences or feelings we have had. They may reveal a positive path through pain or loss that has otherwise gone unnoticed. They may affirm the readers' feelings of gratefulness for gifts received, or demonstrate that we are not alone when our pain is sharp or our anger unresolved. The key is to hear the stories with care and attention. By reading each story as if it is being told by a best friend, a sister or a brother, we receive the most we can from it.

William Carlos Williams, one of America's great poets, had useful advice about listening to other people's stories. Williams was also a full-time physician. As a doctor he believed in the importance of stories. He reminded student doctors that much of their lives as physicians would be spent listening to other people's stories and then trying to help each of them understand the meaning of his or her story. Williams said, "Their story, yours, mine—it's what we all carry with us on this trip we take, and we owe it to each other to respect our stories and learn from them."

About This Series

Saint Mary's Press, as part of its mission to share the Good News with young people, recognizes that young people have much to say about faith. To hear more clearly what young women and men have to say, we initiated this series in 1995 by inviting submissions from students in the United States and Canada.

The first volume, *I Know Things Now: Stories by Teenagers 1*, was published in 1996, followed by *Friends: Stories by Teenagers 2* and *Finding Hope: Stories by Teenagers 3* in 1997 and 1998. To encourage writers to be as honest as possible in telling their stories, they could elect to have their stories printed with their full name, their first name only, or their initials; or they could withhold their name altogether. Those options were also available for this volume.

The range of this collection is remarkable. Through stories of illness, death, and birth, students have clearly and beautifully related their experience of God's presence or absence. Many also sensed God in more commonplace moments and events. But whatever the experience, the writers have expressed themselves courageously, and for this they deserve our heartfelt thanks.

It is a difficult task for an editor to be faced with a wealth of fine material, only to have to put some pieces aside in favor of others. Thanks are also in order for all the students whose stories could not be included here. No story was put aside lightly, and each was read and reviewed with the utmost respect for its writer.

Thanks, too, to the many religion and English teachers all over the country who facilitated the submission of stories from their schools. This book would not have been possible without your help.

Turn the page now and enter the stories—the wonderful, sad, touching, funny ways in which teenagers have come to experience God's presence, and the hard and tragic ways in which some have come to believe that God is absent. Read them alone or with a group; ponder and discuss them; write a story of your own. May these stories remind you of the ways that you, too, can grow in faith.

Katie Luzi
Villa Maria Academy
Malvern, Pennsylvania

Every Step
of the Way

Several years ago I experienced something that I don't tell many people about. It's something close to my heart that has had a great impact on my life.

I was a typical thirteen-year-old girl, loving life and thinking that my loved ones and I could never be hurt by the world around us. I had always prayed, but before this time I prayed only when I needed something or when I had a special intention. And to tell you the truth, I was not placing God first in my life. I had a great boyfriend who promised the world to me. He was my "everything." Friends and popularity also ranked very high. I guess that's a common teenage mistake.

But things began to change. My best friend of eight years started down the wrong path—a path of drugs and destruction—and she got to the point where guys ruled her life and took advantage of her. It felt as if someone had stabbed me in the heart. Seeing her fall apart this way hurt me deeply, but I felt an obligation to stand by her and help her through this tough time.

I knew I had to get out, though, when she began pulling me down with her. I was not about to throw my life away. I was raised to believe in myself, and whenever things got to be intense, I could rely on my family. But things were different this time. I was in denial about the changes going on between my best friend and me. We were supposed to be soul sisters, connected at the hip, but I knew deep in my heart we could never go back.

While all this was going on, I had one person that I fully trusted and loved more than anyone, my boyfriend. He listened, understood, and made me smile when things got bad with my best friend. One day he sat me down and told me he had something very important to tell me. I became scared because I could tell he had been crying. The words that came out of his mouth changed both our lives forever. His dad had just been diagnosed with a brain tumor and had a few short months to live. To make things worse, my boyfriend had to move out of state because his parents wanted to be closer to family during the trying months ahead.

My world changed instantly. I was no longer that happy-go-lucky girl who believed that she was indestructible. For a while I blamed God for allowing my boyfriend's dad to get sick, for the problems between my best friend and me, and for tons of other stuff that wasn't going right. In my eyes my world was falling apart. My grades began to slip, and my parents and I were fighting constantly.

One night it all became too much. I had tons of homework, dance classes all night, I'd just had a fight with my mom, called it quits with my best friend, and my boyfriend had moved away. I felt entirely alone. I ran up to my room, turned off the lights, and lay in my bed, just sobbing and sobbing. I had hit bottom. I said to myself, "I just can't go on like this, it's not worth it." I was feeling so depressed and alone, and I couldn't handle it.

Then as I lay there, I felt a hand on my shoulder—it wasn't a physical hand, it was a force pushing me to sit up in my bed. And as I sat up, I heard a voice in my head say, "It's okay, you can handle it, you're strong." A feeling came over me unlike anything I've ever experienced before—a sense of calmness and comfort that gave me the strength to get out of my bed and deal with my problems slowly and effectively.

I sincerely feel that the force I felt was my guardian angel and the voice was God's. God was telling me that I'll never be alone and that he'll never give me more than I can handle. I have since come closer to God. I can live each day knowing that

God is one of my best friends and will protect me and love me regardless of what happens in my life.

Everything was patched up, and my best friend and I have now gone our separate ways, but I know it's not the end of the world. I have great friends now who support me and love me. Life does go on—I learned that. Life will get hard, I know it will. Some of the hardest years lie straight up ahead, but I know that God will always be there for me, to shine a light on the path I am to follow. As long as I stay true to myself, God will be with me every step of the way.

Megan Smith
Saint Agnes Academy
Memphis, Tennessee

Joseph J. Omlor
Kennedy-Kenrick Catholic
High School
Norristown, Pennsylvania

A Deer in Grandpop's Woods

About a year ago, my grandpop passed away very suddenly of a heart attack. He was seventy-two years old. This was very hard for me to understand. For a while I was mad at God and wanted to know why he took my grandpop, whom I loved very much, away from me. I wondered if I had done something wrong and God was punishing me for it, or if God wanted to test my faith, to see how much of a believer I was. Or maybe it was just time for my grandpop to go to heaven. I don't know.

Grandpop and I were very close. We loved to go fishing and hiking in the woods. He lived in a wooded area; his house had a river right next to it, which is where we did all our fishing together. Grandpop loved to sit on his dock all day catching fish, and even on days when he didn't catch any, he didn't care. He would just go back the next day and try again.

A lot of animals lived around his house. I used to love walking through the woods with Grandpop; we would spend hour after hour looking at all the animals and trees, all of whose names he knew. I would go and visit him once or twice a week, and I would spend all day there Saturday and Sunday. We talked about everything—girls, cars, sports—whatever either of us brought up. He would tell me all about how different things were when he was my age, and how different they would be for me when I got to be his age.

I never got to touch Grandpop or tell him that I loved him before he died, and that made it even harder to understand why he had to leave me. If he had been sick and expected to die soon, that would have made his death easier for me. I would have been ready for it. But because it was so unexpected and no one knew it was going to happen, it was so much harder to understand.

One day when I was visiting his house after he had died, I went for a walk through the woods to see all our favorite places. As I walked I saw a very big deer. I stood still for a while and looked at the deer, and he looked back at me. Then he started to walk toward me. At first I got scared and was about to run, but then I realized that the deer wasn't going to hurt me; he was just seeing what I was doing in his woods. As he came closer, I extended my hand and actually touched the deer right on his head. I rubbed his head for a few seconds, and then he darted off into the woods.

This reminded me of my grandpop, and I felt that God had sent that deer so I would be able to touch my grandpop one last time forever.

Stephanie Pete
Cabrini High School
New Orleans, Louisiana

A Little Gracious Gift from God

My family seemed complete eight years ago, with two dogs, my little brother, my mom and dad, and of course me, the princess of the household. What else could we ask for? So needless to say, I couldn't understand why my mom was so ecstatic when she announced that she was expecting another baby. At least I couldn't understand it until she burst into the house one day with a picture of the unborn baby. She had had an ultrasound, and the nurse gave her a picture of the baby. Seeing this unborn baby was unbelievable and amazing. My mom exclaimed, "It's a boy!" Now I was so excited to have a new baby brother on the way. I couldn't wait for him to be born. I watched the calendar, hoping that July 3, 1990, would hurry up and get here.

In February, though, the preparations for the new baby were put on hold. My mom wasn't feeling well, so my dad brought her to the doctor. They were gone a long time. My dad finally came home with the glum news. He sat my brother and me on the sofa and started to tell us the bad news. "Your mom's water bag broke and the baby will probably die." I was only eight years old, and my brother was only five, so we didn't quite understand. My dad explained that if the baby was born now, they would not attempt to save the baby. My mom was only twenty weeks pregnant, and they do not attempt to save babies until they are at least twenty-four weeks. This was very upsetting to my parents, because on the ultrasound you could see a

19

very active, fully formed baby moving around. The doctors told my mom that she would deliver within forty-eight hours and that the baby would die. They tried to persuade her into aborting the baby at that moment. They thought this would be the easiest way to go. But she refused. I guess the doctors didn't know my mom's faith in God and her strength to conquer anything that faces her in life.

My mom was in the hospital for eight weeks before she started to have contractions. Every day the doctor would come in and shake his head in disbelief. At twenty-eight weeks the baby was born, and he had a chance to survive. The doctors told my parents that the new baby would not cry because his lungs would not be mature enough, but they were wrong. The baby cried so loud that my parents could hear him from the other room. They had to put him on a ventilator to help out his lungs. After two hours a nurse went to my mom's room and said that although their new son had a big mountain to climb, things were looking good. We all kept praying and thanking God for our miracle baby.

My mom was able to go home two days later. But before she could leave, they had to choose a name for the baby. A nurse brought my parents a book of names and meanings. They decided on the name "Paul John" because Paul means "little" and John means "God's gracious gift." We all agreed that he was a little gracious gift from God.

I recall visiting Paul in the hospital. He looked so small, especially with the tubes they had to put in him. I couldn't wait till he would be well enough to come home. They said he should be able to come home in July. Well, Paul John climbed that mountain very quickly. He had his share of problems, but he conquered every one of them and was able to come home on May thirtieth, much sooner than anticipated.

He weighed only four pounds when he came home. I was so excited. We passed this tiny child around from person to person. I can still remember dressing him up in my baby-doll clothes. Having another baby brother was great. Paul was always the happiest baby. He laughed and smiled all the time. He learned and discovered new things. He even discovered the scar where he'd had a feeding tube in his belly. He thought it was his second belly button.

Although Paul John slipped on many rocks on his way up, he has made it all the way to the top of the mountain. God was with Paul every step of the way. My mom always says, whenever Paul runs into an obstacle, that God put him on this earth for a reason. I know that God, through his presence in Paul, has given this family more than anyone could ask for. He is our reminder that with God by our side, we can conquer anything. When we forget the important things, we step back and take a long look at our little miracle.

My family is complete now with three dogs, one cat, my two little brothers, my mom and dad, and of course me. I am now queen of the family. Paul is seven years old, and he shows off his second belly button to his friends. Paul John Pete is a miracle baby and is our family's little gracious gift from God.

A Journey to Grasp the Light Inside Me

Becky Bennett
Santa Clara High School
Oxnard, California

A sudden burst of the morning sun capped the tall trees of the forest. Droplets of dew prismed the sun into a world that was hidden. There is nothing really there except for nature and the feelings of fullness and love. A certain presence drifts through the sky and fills every creature, along with me, with a sense of lovingness. Things were not always this peaceful, I tell you. There was another place that used to be filled with war, fear, and emptiness. I welcome you to my former world.

In a place where the sun never shone and you had only a star to light your way, I hid fearfully in the crevices. A fear of what? Everything. People mostly, the people that tortured me for most of my life and put me down when I couldn't feel any lower. My parents never could understand me. I could always escape to the forest beyond all this war, but it would be a long journey. It would be a journey to test my strength, willpower, and faith. Deep down I knew I could do it, but it seemed easier to stay where I was and just let everything happen. I am, however, an adventurer, always wanting to do dangerous things and meet death face-to-face. I was up for the challenge, but I didn't know if I could handle it. It seemed odd for me to yell for help, but suddenly I didn't have to. Someone stood before me, straight and graceful. I looked up, and he spoke, "I am here for you. I always have been and always will be." Just as suddenly as he appeared, he no longer stood there.

Standing in awe at what happened, I heard a noise that became louder and louder. It sounded like a siren, but when it exploded several feet from me, I knew that I had to decide. I made my decision and made a dash for the outskirts of town, avoiding bombs, explosions, deaths, the destruction of a city, and the destruction of my heart and the hope of a young girl who was leaving her only home behind.

As I was running, a man grabbed me out of the darkness and pulled me off the streets. "Hey, listen, if you want to get out of this town, I'll help you. But you'll have to do me a huge favor. I'll make sure that you'll be well-rewarded with anything in this world that you want." I thought about it, considering the possibilities. I realized that this was one of the temptations in my life. I decided what to do, and kicked the man really hard. He sprawled over in pain and muttered some words. I took the chance and ran as far away as I could. I soon grew tired and slowed down.

With chin held high and eyes fighting back hot tears, I reached the edge of town. I took a breath and stepped into the forest. Cool air hit my face like a blast, and the sights before me made me stand in awe. Before me endless green fields unfolded, and the brilliant sun sparked the blue sky. The stream was clean and clear, with little pebbles glittering in the afternoon sun. I turned to look back at my world and saw that everything was falling apart. I wouldn't think about that now. I had a friend that was always looking out for me. I was to make new decisions, new friends, and take a new look at life. A voice echoed in my head, saying: "In the destruction of the city, I placed a little light, a little glimmer of hope, in the sky. It lit your way on your journey here, and now it is sunny. I am your light."

Then a sudden burst of the morning sun capped the tall trees of the forest, and droplets of dew prismed the sun into a world that was hidden.

Christopher Beaver
Kennedy-Kenrick Catholic
High School
Norristown, Pennsylvania

This Praying Business

There I am playing Wheel of Fortune on an Apple II in the computer classroom during the first grade. The time on the clock reads 2:23, and I'm getting nervous. "Car riders and walkers" (my dismissal call) has just echoed over the P.A., and I'm watching a computerized Vanna White turn over a "w" in the object "washing machine." Other kids are doing likewise, though some have opted for the then-incomprehensible "Where in the World Is Carmen San Diego?"

Eventually the teacher dismisses us, and we run to our classrooms on the next floor down. Books fly in and out of my Optimus Prime Transformers schoolbag ten seconds before I run through the front door of the building. When I get out there, I am greeted by a parking lot in which the most noteworthy thing for me is the absence of my mom's car. Nor are any of the people present that my mom drove home in those days. It becomes quite evident to me that my mom has hung me out to dry. However, let's straighten something out here. My mom isn't a bad person. She just thought I had walked home, because my house is just around the block. Understand, back when you are seven years old, things like that ruin a kid's week. I once saw a dead bird while riding my three-wheeler: scarred for life.

The next day in religion class, my teacher said something I wouldn't forget: Jesus, Mary, and the whole cast of characters like to hear prayers, especially from children. Even to this day I do not understand the logistics of this, especially the point that they (the heavenly responders) hold children's prayers in special regard; I mean, it can't be because children have the most problems. It is probably because adults think children will buy anything they sell. (Just look at the multimillion-dollar children's cereal industry: poor product, indeed!) Yet I was desperate; I didn't want to miss my ride again, so I took a shot at this praying business.

Same situation that day. My sharp-as-clay teacher didn't realize it was time to pack up and haul on out until car riders and walkers was announced. I am downstairs in an instant, books in the bag, and I walk out to a parking lot filled with cars.

Of course this "phenomenon" can be attributed to the flow of things in my grade school. You see, certain students in the seventh grade were awarded the honor of opening the doors for the students on my floor. Now, their job was supposed to be to open the doors and hold them open when car riders and walkers was called. Of course they didn't do this. Seventh graders take great joy in tormenting younger kids who see freedom beyond the older punks. So the seventh graders hold the doors shut until anarchy is about to break out among the younger students. On that day I just ran by them.

The fact is you don't judge God's action by general merit but by the significance to the individual involved. For me, getting out in time for my ride that day was my first experience with God, but just like first impressions, it is that first experience that means the most to me. I would later in life feel God's touch in a greater fashion, but it is that first time that sticks in my mind the most.

Allison Hodges
Immaculate Heart Academy
Westwood, New Jersey

Playing House with Jessica

I have felt a strong sense of God's presence many times in my life. However, one experience stands out in my mind as the time when I most clearly and distinctly saw the face of God. In preparation for my Confirmation, I performed many service projects, including a trip to the Tomorrow's Children Foundation at Hackensack Hospital.

The Tomorrow's Children Foundation is a special wing of Hackensack Hospital made exclusively for children with cancer. It is specially designed to accommodate children with all forms of cancer and to facilitate their treatment and care. The rooms are bright and beautiful and help to welcome and calm the children. A colorful waiting area has everything from stickers and construction paper to dolls and trucks. Vivid pictures and posters adorn the multicolored walls, and works of art by children hang from the ceiling. Each child is known here by name.

I had chosen this service project because it seemed to be the easiest and the one requiring the least amount of effort on my part. I was definitely not aware of what I was getting myself into. My job as a volunteer was to stay in the waiting area and play with the children as they came in for treatment or were recovering from recent operations. Mrs. Keane, who was in charge of the service projects in my parish at the time, told us that our main responsibility was to keep a happy face even though we may see some sad or disturbing things. So even though it seemed like an easy project, I was not looking forward to spending my time with these children. I was afraid that I wouldn't know how to react to them and their illnesses and that I wouldn't be helping them at all. I went there not knowing what to expect.

When I got there, however, things were not as bad as I thought they would be. The place was bright and cheery, and the kids looked like normal children. They were so adorable! Everyone wanted to play something different, and I had trouble keeping up with them. However, my fun ended when I looked over to see Jessica, a little five-year-old, sitting by herself in the corner of the room. She looked so sad, and tears filled her eyes as she sat watching everyone else play. I went over to her, but she quickly crossed her arms and turned her back to me. Feeling a little discouraged, I came up to her and asked her if she would like to play. She shook her head no and turned away again. After a few minutes of suggestions, I finally asked her if she wanted to play house with me. With a sudden burst of excitement, she ran from her chair, grabbed a doll from the shelf, and came running back to me. She wanted to pretend that she was a mother and was bringing her baby into the hospital for chemotherapy.

Naturally I was surprised by how much she knew about chemotherapy and intravenous treatments. She must have spent a lot of time in the hospital. We played together for at least two hours, and when it was time for me to leave, she started to cry and attached herself to my leg. I felt really bad about leaving her because I felt connected to her in a way. With tears in my own eyes, I left the hospital. Mrs. Keane later asked me about my experience. When I told her that Jessica and I had played for almost the entire time I was there, she looked amazed. In all the time that she had been sending volunteers to the Tomorrow's Children Foundation, she told me, Jessica had never spoken to anyone.

I truly felt that God played a big part in my success as a volunteer at Tomorrow's Children Foundation. He helped me make a difference in one little girl's life, and that was all I needed to turn from an apathetic participant to an active volunteer.

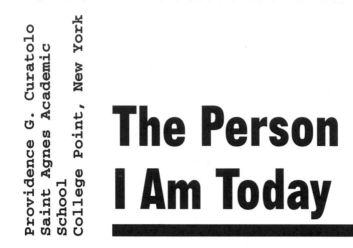

Providence G. Curatolo
Saint Agnes Academic
School
College Point, New York

The Person I Am Today

Hello. My name is Providence Curatolo. I am fifteen years old, born on July 1, 1982. I have lived a hard and challenging life. I have been reminded many times of God's presence in my life. I have also had times in my life when I felt that God was nowhere near me, or didn't even exist. But each hardship I have gone through has only helped me grow spiritually, emotionally, and mentally, making me stronger and bringing me closer to God.

I would like to share an experience with you, one of the hardest times in my life, but one in which I felt God's presence the most. And so I begin from the beginning of this hard journey.

I had just returned home from Florida with my sister, Cathie. She had won two tickets in a singing contest, and I used the second ticket. It was the summer of fourth grade going into fifth grade for me. While we were on vacation, I had experienced a slight pain in my stomach. I rested a bit and then the pain was gone. I didn't feel it again for the rest of the trip. Not until I got home.

A few days went by. One night I was laying in my bed, and as I breathed in, I had a sudden pain again in my stomach, except this time it was worse. The only way I can describe what I was feeling is that every time I took a breath, it felt like one, two, three bubbles would form one within the other, and as I exhaled, all of them would pop. I thought it might pass if I went to sleep.

In the morning the bubbles were still forming, but they weren't as painful. I remember that during the night, I had gone into my parents' room and put myself between them. I told them about the pain I was feeling. My dad, Joe, brought me into my room and told me to do the sign of the cross, say my prayers, and I would feel better when I woke up. I listened, but the pain did not go away.

Days went by and the pain got worse, but I felt as if my parents did not believe me. I described the bubbles to them. I found out later that the reason they did not take me to the doctor was that they thought I was getting my period.

One day my mom, Rose, sent me to the store to get milk. I remember saying that I didn't feel well, but she told me not to be lazy. I took the money and began to walk to the corner store, which usually takes about forty seconds at the most. I was in so much pain that I was bending forward, holding my stomach. I was crying so much, but I couldn't shout or scream because I didn't have the energy. I wondered why the neighbors did not come to help me. When I got to the store, my brother's girl-friend was there. She saw me and came to my aid right away. I could not stand up straight. She started to walk me home, but saw I was not going to make it, so she ran to my house and got my brother, Santo, who came to walk with me, too.

When I got home, I told my mom, sarcastically, that I was just lying about feeling sick. She still didn't completely believe me. No one really believed me until we arrived at First Med, where the doctor, as soon as he saw my stomach, said that he needed to rush me to Schneider Children's Hospital for a burst appendix. I was frightened and thought I would die. It turned out to be not a burst appendix but a tumor. I had surgery on August 7. Before the doctors could get to the tumor, two liters of water had to be removed. Behind that water was an eight-pound tumor. They said that I would get better within a few days, and I would need to get a checkup in a few weeks.

Three weeks later we returned to the hospital. They asked us many questions and took my parents, my sister, and me into a small room. They started throwing around some big scientific words. Words like "malignant" and "benign" cancer cells. They said that these things were in my body. I heard my mom and sister crying softly. My father, like me, was confused. Then I heard the one statement that completely frightened me: "You will lose your hair. You have ovarian cancer." After hearing these words, I ran out of the room, and my sister came after me. I was so nervous, and my tears just wouldn't stop.

My parents decided to get a second opinion at Memorial Sloan-Kettering. When we got there the next day, something inside me said that this was a good place for me to be. I met my doctor. She explained what I would need to go through, and I decided to choose this hospital. I was told that I would need four months of chemotherapy.

Four months turned out to be six instead. I was only ten years old. In those six months, I went through so much pain. I wouldn't eat. I mostly slept. When I lost my hair, I lost some of my will to live. I became very sad. I felt so bad for myself. Part of me wanted to live, but part of me also wanted to die and get out of all this pain. I had so many operations and surgeries and different types of transfusions. My body was weak. I wanted so much just to stay in bed, but my family would not allow it. They would not let me give up, as much as I wanted nature to take its course. The days I wanted to give up were the days that I felt God the strongest. On those days I would fight the strongest and the hardest, because God gave me the strength.

God has given me a second chance to live my life, and to live it well. Because of God's presence in my life, I decided that I would fight this battle to the end. All through this experience, God was with me, giving me the strength and the motivation to live and to get up every day and fight. I got my victory. I survived. I conquered the cancer. It took its toll on my body, but there was no way I would let it break my soul. I have been blessed with this situation. Without it I would not be the person I am today. I have gained a respect for people. No matter what disability someone may have, I know that each of them has a soul. I care for everyone. I know that if I had not had the cancer, I would not be as caring as I am today. I thank God for his presence in my life. All the times I have fallen, God has raised me back up. I am grateful to God for my life, and I plan to live a very full and happy one.

Veronica Molina
Trinity High School
Garfield, Ohio

Brad Amiri
Duchesne High School
Saint Charles, Missouri

Transcendence

There is no definitive proof of God's existence, yet many people base their whole lives on religions that have God at the center. Believers develop faith in God even though they cannot see, hear, or touch God physically. The presence of God can be easily questioned, but it can also be easily defended. I have questioned the presence of God, something everyone has to do at one time or another. The most important experience of God's presence for me occurred through the sacrament of Confirmation.

At my school, the eighth-grade class celebrates Confirmation. I went to Mass three times a week, not always willingly. My class and I had to do service hours and cram as much information about the religion of Catholicism into our brains as we could. We never really thought of God as a loving Father; we said it all the time, but never took the time to stop and think about what it meant. When I prayed, I talked. That is all I did, because I was not really talking to God. Mass became boring and seemed to have no point, even though I knew that the Eucharist was the biggest celebration in Catholicism.

The day of Confirmation came, and I was about to receive the Holy Spirit and agree, in God's presence, that I wanted to be a Catholic. I was nervous along with my classmates as we realized we had been preparing for this one night the whole year and that the bishop was really here. Praying, responding, and singing during the celebration, I began to discover what it was like to participate in the Mass. After I received the blessing, I felt different. A moment of transcendence came to me, and I felt warm, knowing that I shared the feeling of love with God.

After I was confirmed, I changed dramatically. I found myself wanting to go to church to receive new strength from the body and blood of Jesus. The Scriptures and the facts about religion that I learned in grade school became meaningful and taught lessons of life. The Gospels were not just stories but the actual history of the revelation of God's Son. Praying was a gift that I began using more frequently, and I found that my prayers were answered more often. The whole idea that God loved me and suffered for me became a reality.

The doubting stage was what developed my strong faith in God. Now I see that there is enough evidence for me to live my life for an unseen God. When I look at the universe or anything, I recognize God's presence—the only other explanation for its existence is by happenstance, which is illogical. My new perception of the world and my faith and friendship with God can be explained only by the Holy Spirit, God's eternal presence.

Laura Kay Slavicek
Lake Michigan Catholic
High School
Saint Joseph, Michigan

Lesson Number One

I've been going out with Ryan for five-and-a-half months, but recently I've felt at a loss about what to do with him. Now don't get me wrong—he's a wonderful and caring person, but he has his faults like everyone else. Unfortunately his problems are serious: low self-esteem and a serious lack of self-confidence. However, I see the potential in him, and I try to foster that. I could see he wasn't happy with the way his life was, so I asked him what he thought he should change. I didn't get an answer. That's when I knew something was missing in his life. After all, if someone has never been exposed to something, how are they to know it exists?

Ryan has told me that he is jealous of the life I lead. I don't think my life is much to be jealous about, but I tried to see things from his point of view. I thought of the differences between Ryan's life and mine, and I came up with one major contrast: religion. I go to church every Sunday with my family and have a strong faith in God. Ryan doesn't go to church. His parents have never pushed religion, and he doesn't really know what to make of God. The connection I made was between loving God and therefore loving yourself, and having high self-esteem and self-confidence. Ryan has come with me to church before, but I suspect it was just to be with me and didn't have that much to do with hearing the word of God. I decided to put my theory to the test.

"Ryan," I began, "can I ask you a question?"

"Of course," he replied.

"Would you like to learn more about God and about going to church?" I asked hesitantly. I was hesitant because I am Catholic, and frequently people shy away from the supposed rigidness of Catholicism. I grew up as a Catholic, so it doesn't bother me, but I knew enough not to force my beliefs on Ryan. I wanted him to decide on his own and not say yes just to make me happy. However, Ryan surprised me.

"Yes," he answered.

"Ryan," I said, "think about this. Do you seriously want to learn about God?"

"Yes," he assured me. "I've always wanted to go to church and learn about God and stuff, but no one would ever take me. My parents never took me to church, and nobody else ever would."

I looked into his eyes and knew he was telling the truth. I wrapped him in a bear hug, and at that moment, I felt a force surging through my body. It was a sensation I'd never felt before. I had energy and felt like I could do anything. Also, inside me was this feeling of indescribable happiness that I could express only by crying my eyes out. Then I had another insight: it was not only me, it was us. The feeling I had was flowing between the two of us; it was us. It was our bond, and then I knew it was God's presence in our bond. Without a doubt God was with us in that room.

"Ryan," I said. "You may think I'm crazy, but God is in us right now."

He looked into my eyes, and I could see God in him. I burst into tears all over again, releasing my joy in a flood. I knew then and there that I was doing a good thing and that it was the right thing. Ryan was crying too, and we hugged each other tight. I don't know if he is the person I will spend the rest of my life with, but we will always share a close bond because of this experience. It is a bond no one can break because it is a bond with each other and with God.

Even though this happened only a few days ago, I can see a change in Ryan. He is more concerned with the direction of his life, and he is eager to learn how he can change for the better.

The first step has already been taken, and that is to admit that something needs to be changed. I gave Ryan lesson number one in religion: God loves us unconditionally. I explained to him what it means and wrote it down for him so that he can read it whenever he needs to. I told him he can talk to me whenever he needs to and that we will go to church soon. I wanted to go this Sunday, but unfortunately I have to play my flute at church, so I wouldn't be able to sit with Ryan. I don't want him to have to sit alone in church, because we are in this together; I don't want him to feel he is alone.

We're going to Mass Saturday night.

Erica Colón
Bishop Loughlin Memorial
High School
Brooklyn, New York

Wishes and Fears

My best friend, Manny, used to tell me that dreams were the wishes of a person's subconscious, and that nightmares were his or her fears. He described a nightmare he'd had the night before about dying, but I didn't really get the meaning behind it except to think that he was afraid of death. Now as I stand here on the beach, my black wide-leg slacks flying in the breeze, I laugh to think of how dense I am. I just finished giving the eulogy at his funeral.

Manny was a daredevil. His dream wedding was to shout "I do!" while jumping out of a plane without a parachute, and have his bride catch him while she opened hers. He said it was the only way he'd be able to trust his bride. I told him no sane woman would go through that, and, laughing, he said that sane women were the bane of his existence. We'd have talks like that while driving to this very beach on his secondhand Harley, and I'd take pictures of him while he'd do his mixture of Chinese meditation and karate, called *kata*. We spent so much time together here that it feels strange to be here without him. I feel almost as if I left my right arm in the car, or in the church.

I was the first person his mother called after he was shot, hit by a stray bullet. I still hear the moans coming from his little sister after hearing the doctors say that Manny had slipped into a coma from which he might never emerge. Six days later he was pronounced brain dead, and I can still feel his hand on mine as the doctors turned off his life support. Throughout all this I never cried—not even once. I think I was too weak to bring even one teardrop, let alone the river my heart was crying. I was also the only person standing during the service, right at the head of his casket. I was thinking, "Why are we here?" Wondering, as I spoke, why I was mourning the death of a seventeen-year-old boy. What kind of God is there in heaven that would take the life of someone who hadn't really begun yet to live?

I'm still thinking of that, even as I remove my boots and the thin socks I have on beneath them. I feel the waves rush over my feet, and it's probably cold, but I can't tell. My whole body feels cold, and I can't feel the sun, even though it's been out in full force. Wow, I must have been here for a while! The sun is getting ready to set. I stand still, the ocean soaking the bottoms of my slacks, and I stare at the majestic heavens that now embrace the soul of my best friend. A breeze blows and dries the tears I didn't even know were there.

So dreams are our subconscious wishes, and nightmares our fears? What I make of this now is that God grants us the power to make our dreams come true. Yet only he can make our nightmares a reality.

Rebecca Bishop
Our Lady of Good Counsel
High School
Wheaton, Maryland

Charlie Binger
Lake Michigan Catholic
High School
Saint Joseph, Michigan

Sage

August twentieth, my first day of work, and the Brew Pub felt cold and empty. The inside was shattered and looked destroyed. The next two weeks would be spent putting pieces together and preparing for the future. It was a lonely place with a sad atmosphere. As I stood alone dusting, I heard a voice from behind me.

"Hi, my name is Sage, Sage Mallet."

"Hi, I'm Charlie," I replied.

A kind and gentle-looking individual stood beside me. His face radiated joy and happiness. His big brown eyes welcomed me. As we worked, we discussed the simple aspects of life. He told me how he was going to name his kid Rubber, as in "Rubber Mallet." He had an innocence and charm to him. I worked for a couple of months with Sage. We became close friends and great workers. Together we could accomplish any task. Sage fit in perfectly with all my friends. We began hanging out on weekends. We went to pool halls and campfires and laughed through every minute of it.

In late October, on a Wednesday, I was heading to work. I was looking forward to work because Sage was also scheduled to be there. When I arrived, a waitress asked me if I wanted to contribute money for Sage's family.

Confused, I asked, "What happened to Sage's family?"

Her mouth hung open, and she whimpered, "You didn't hear?"

"Hear what?" I asked.

"Last night when Sage was heading home . . ."

My eyes began to water and my knees got weak. She finished the story of how Sage had gotten into a head-on car accident and died. My face was pale, and my heart stopped. Each breath was a struggle to take. She asked if I was all right. I answered simply, "Fine," and proceeded to the bathroom where I wept quietly alone. The room seemed cold and lonely.

At Sage's funeral I spoke with another friend from work. I gave him a hug and said, "Hey." He told me something surprising and troublesome. He said, "You know, Sage was telling me the other day how much he was looking forward to going to your February-first party." I'll never forget that statement, and I'll never forget Sage.

Some people would lose faith in God over this incident. Others would use God for support. I don't know what role God played. I do know that Sage was sixteen when he was killed. He'll never be able to name his kid Rubber. The last thing Sage said to me was, "See ya later." Can you imagine if you never again saw the last person who said that to you?

Amanda L. Bolender
Archbishop Curley-Notre
Dame High School
Miami, Florida

Kim

On May 28, 1997, one of my best friends died suddenly.

Wednesday, on the way to school with a friend, we saw a big accident. We couldn't actually see the car, but we did see a white van, a car, police cars, people, and a fire truck. Of course I thought little of it. I felt bad that there was an accident, but that was about all.

I arrived at school a little late, but things seemed normal. I came out of the locker room and started walking to where Kim usually was, but someone came up and told me Kim had been in an accident. The bell rang and everyone went to class. I felt confused, wondering if the accident I had seen earlier could have involved Kim.

I went to my first-period class. Still no one knew anything about the accident. About twenty minutes later, Caroline came to the door to talk to Mr. Morril and me because she had found out for sure that Kim Lacek was hurt and in the hospital.

I didn't really understand what was going on. When I went back in the classroom and sat down, I just started crying. Then I went to the bathroom, hoping the walk would calm me down.

Third period I had P.E., and because Kim was usually in that class with me, and she wasn't there, I couldn't help but cry. Nothing was normal after everyone found out about the accident. Then Heather came in, crying her eyes out, with the news:

Kim didn't make it. I didn't know what to do or think. I tried to hold myself together, but I started crying.

All I could think was, "Why? Why to her? Why did God have to take such a good person? Kim was such a sweet, loving person, an honor student, a good daughter, a good sister, pretty, and a good friend. What will I do without her?" The only person who could answer that question was God. But at this point I really didn't want to have anything to do with God.

Our whole freshman class was excused from school for the rest of the day, but that night there was a memorial for Kim at the site of the crash. Channel 10 News was there interviewing people who knew Kim. People wanted me to go to the interviewer, but I didn't because I didn't think I could handle it.

Everything at school was so different and weird. To this day things are still different and weird. I often want to call her and tell her my problems and whatever else is going on; then I realize she isn't there to call anymore. I knew God was with me, but I really didn't want him to be. I think I felt this way because God just took the life of one of my friends, and it wasn't fair to anyone. I wanted her back, and so did a lot of other people; but apparently God wanted her, too.

I couldn't sleep until after the viewing. That was the first time I had slept a full night since the accident. The viewing had been difficult because Kim just didn't look like herself; she was wearing an outfit in her casket that she would never have chosen herself. I felt as if this was a really bad nightmare, and I wanted to wake up.

At the viewing the priest said, "Kim was a gift from God, and he thought it was time for her to go." I thought that was wrong; that would mean that God is an Indian giver. All during the service, I was expecting her to just jump up as if the whole death were a joke.

My family tried to help me as much as I would let them, which was not very much. At this time I only wanted to be with my friends; I didn't know if I would lose another one. Paul Alexander was the person who helped me the most. Paul and I hadn't been very close, but after Kim's death we became very close friends.

I heard God was with me because everyone was telling me so, but after the funeral I didn't want to have anything to do with God. I didn't understand how God could put a child's death on so many people. Everything that I had been taught in the past fourteen years of my life was fading away fast. I still have my doubts about God and religions. I don't understand why God does things that hurt people so much in so many ways. I am even farther away from religion than I ever have been. Inside I really don't feel as if God is with me. Maybe I don't want him to be, but I don't know the answer for myself right now.

A Warm Blanket of Love

K. B.
Saint Barnabas
High School
Bronx, New York

Hi. I would like to let you know what to expect from my story. I am not going to preach to you or make myself seem "holier than thou." In fact, I'm as far as possible from that. I am just a normal sixteen-year-old in her junior year of high school. My simple wish is to share with you an experience that was life-changing for me, one that enlightened my mind and my soul. This is the story of how I found God.

God set out for me long before I had even a remote inkling of it. I was born into a Christian family and raised believing the Gospel of Jesus. Church was the centerpiece of family life, and I know I loved God for as far back as I can remember. In Florida, where I lived, I enjoyed every minute of my life. Life was good; it couldn't have been better. Yet all of a sudden, like a thunderstorm, what was once a picturesque life became as dramatic as a caption straight out of a Batman and Robin film. I could feel that something not-so-good was about to happen, but at the time, the innocence of my youth prevented me from seeing the rather adult reason why.

It began with Mommy and Daddy arguing a lot. Then my big sister got a new boyfriend, and that made for even more quarrels. Things weren't as pleasant as they had been. However, being only ten years old, I just played with my dolls and ignored the whole thing. "It'll pass. They're just grouchy." Or so I thought.

Soon Dad and Mom stopped fighting. Now that I look back on the whole situation, I realize they had stopped talking altogether. After a while Daddy went to Jamaica (my homeland) for a visit—an extended visit. Big Sis went away to college, and Mommy started working even more. I, on the other hand, was in ignorant bliss. Why, I finally had my own room. I could wear whatever clothes my sister left that fit me, and I was in H-E-A-V-E-N. Well, that was the shortest eternity I ever spent! Before I knew it, there was a sign outside my house that read "For Sale," and the next thing I knew, I was on a plane to New York.

Things were changing rapidly, and I was very confused. "Dear God, please bless my family and old friends. Please let the kids in my new school be nice to me, and oh, please let my new house be pretty. Amen." I was still a baby.

Two years down the road, I was living in a Bronx apartment with two bedrooms and one bathroom (one bathroom, oh, the horror), my body was changing, and so was my personality. I was mad all the time. There was a piece of me missing, but I wasn't sure where I'd lost it.

Things just didn't make sense anymore. My family had grown, and included three new souls. Life was hard. We were constantly on the move, and all the stability of my childhood was slipping through my fingers. It just seemed like everything and everyone around me was in a whirlwind of change, and I was left there with my head spinning. I began questioning God's love. Why had he abandoned us? I prayed for better times, but he never answered me. Why wasn't God listening?

Now for all you soap-opera fans out there, I'm sorry to say that this won't be the sad story of a good girl turned drug addict or gang member. It's just a story of the loss of a simple heart. Yes, that was it, my innocent love for God was being tested. "Dear Lord," I prayed, "please make me a better person— for you."

Weeks passed after that prayer. I didn't hear an answer. Then one hot summer morning, I was awakened (no, not by a bright light) by the sound of my mother shouting and the two babies wrecking the apartment. I felt overwhelmed by it all. I slithered onto my knees and poured my heart out to God. Then

I went back to sleep. That's when it happened. There was no magic dust or sparkles, nor did an angel appear to me, but something much better, something priceless. I felt a warm blanket of love wrap around me, and I felt God tell me not to worry, to let my heart be still, and that he loved me.

No magic show, no drug, nothing of this world could match that feeling. That summer day God gave me a hug and told me he loved me. No, my life is not perfect now and my problems have not disappeared, but I know that God loves me, and that makes all the difference.

Danny Brosnahan
Saint John the Baptist
Diocesan High School
West Islip, New York

Answered Prayers

It was a regular Saturday morning. The sun was shining and it was warm. I knew that my mom had gone to the doctor, but I didn't know why. When my mom finally got home, she had a weird look on her face and in her eyes. She looked like something was wrong and that she had something to tell me. I asked her where she had been. She asked if I remembered a time before then when she had gone to the doctor. I told her that I remembered, and I asked her if this was about the same thing and she said that it was. You see, last time she went to the doctor, it was about something on her neck. The next thing she told me would change my life. She told me that she had cancer.

The weather seemed to change the moment she told me she had cancer. A million things rushed through my mind at that moment. I asked her if she was serious. I just couldn't believe it. She assured me that she'd be all right. She said that she had to go to the hospital for surgery, and that the doctors would be able to remove the cancer. That made me feel a little better, but there was still a tremendous weight on my shoulders. For days that was all I could think about. I wanted my mom to be all right. It was still so hard to believe what was happening. Every day when I went to school, I asked them to pray for my mom in the announcements. Every day I prayed for my mom, prayed that she would be all right. Finally the day came that my mom had to go to the hospital for surgery. I was so worried about

49

her. I prayed for the surgery to go okay. When I got home from school the next day, my dad told me that the surgery had gone okay and that we could visit her.

I absolutely hate going to visit people in the hospital, so you can imagine how I felt visiting my mom. We were standing outside my mom's room and I couldn't wait to see her, but I didn't know what to expect. I had no idea what she would look like after having surgery. We walked into my mom's room and I saw her lying in the bed. She had a big bandage on her neck and she was half awake. I really hated seeing her like this. Then my mom turned and smiled at me. At that moment I experienced the presence of God. A tremendous weight was lifted off my shoulders. I prayed every day, and my prayers were answered. My mom was okay.

Alison Rusan-Long
Saint Elizabeth Academy
Saint Louis, Missouri

Everything Happens for a Reason

There was a time when I thought God was absent in my life, and I did not know what I was going to do. It was in June of 1996, when I was running on a summer track-and-field team. I did not really care for my coach, Marshall Clark, and he didn't really care that I didn't care for him. Every day I would get so mad at him, but the madder I got, the less he cared.

I can deal with a little hard work, but I am not into being trained like a soldier in the army. I had never worked so hard in my whole life. The first day after practice, I thought that I was dead, but I went back for more torture. Every time I would complain, Coach Clark would say, "Shut up and run." I would say, "You get out here and run." I literally hated Coach Clark, and thought he was the meanest man alive.

There were times when we would laugh and joke, but when Coach said run, you better run. The things that I said about Coach were terrible and, to this very day, I regret them, because I know he only wanted the best for me.

One day I got so mad after practice, I told my mom that I was not running anymore because I didn't feel that it was for me. The Sunday after I quit, Coach called my mom and they talked for a long time on the phone about my decision to quit the team. He didn't feel it was a good decision, and he talked my mom into making me go back because he said that I had potential and that if I worked hard, I could be good. When my mom told me that I had to go back, I was not too happy about it, but I got over it.

After deciding to rejoin the team, I called Coach to let him know that I would be there for the next practice on Tuesday. He was not home, so I left the message with his son Chris. The next day my mom picked me up from school, but for some reason I cannot remember, I had to call my sister at home first. When she answered the phone, before I could even say anything, she told me Coach had been killed in a car accident. I didn't believe her. I said, "That's not funny, Averi." But she was dead serious. I became totally numb and kept on saying, "I cannot believe this, cannot believe this."

The night before, Coach had gone to a graduation for a boy he had coached and who had become like another son to him. You see, the boy didn't have a father, and Coach was the only father that he ever knew. After the graduation there was a party; he left the party later on that night and started to head home. Because Coach was a busy man, he did get tired. I guess this time he got a little too tired and could not stay awake. While he was driving down the highway, he fell asleep at the wheel and hit a wall; the rest is pretty self-explanatory.

That night Coach Marshall Clark was taken away from lots of people who not only loved him but also respected him. After I found out what had happened, I couldn't sleep, and all I thought about was Coach and how I wanted to hear him tell me one more time, "Girl, shut up and run."

I didn't want to go to the funeral, but my daddy and I went. After it was over, I was glad that we had gone. At the funeral people got up and told stories about Coach and how much he had meant to them. There were so many people whose lives he had touched and who said that they would never forget him. When the funeral was coming to an end, it was time for everyone to say their last good-byes to Coach. I remember walking by the casket, crying and saying good-bye: "I love you, and I promise to keep running." I knew that the person I was looking at wasn't the man I knew, but I know that he was up in heaven and that he heard what I said.

One of the best things about Coach was his million-dollar smile. Coach had a smile that could light up the whole universe, and it would stay like that forever. I used to wonder how a man that I had thought was so mean could have a smile like that. It was not a normal smile; it was a smile that God gives only to really special people. I wonder why God had to take away a man who was so special to so many people. I guess God had a reason for doing it, but I'm just now seeing that.

I run track for my school now, and before every meet I talk to Coach and ask him to help me do the best I can. When I start complaining and want to stop running, I hear Coach just as loud as day saying, "Girl, shut up and run!" When it is my turn to receive the baton on my relay team, I talk to Coach; it is kind of like he's talking back to me, and the more he talks, the faster I run. This may sound crazy, but as I'm handing the baton off to my teammate, I hear him telling me, "I knew you had it in you."

For a while I thought God was absent in my life because I had said all those bad things about Coach, and before I could really talk to him again, he was gone. I still do not know why God took such a good man off this earth, but I'm sure there was a good reason. One thing I know is that God helps me with a lot of things in my life, but no one helps me and keeps me running as fast as I can more than a man by the name of Coach Marshall Clark!

Mat Hickling
Bishop Dennis J.
O'Connell
High School
Arlington, Virginia

A. T. F.
Bishop Grimes High School
East Syracuse, New York

My Best Chance

God was in my life even before I was born. My biological mother and grandmother decided that the best option for me was adoption. My biological mother realized that there was no way she could truly take care of me, and because she really did love me, she decided to give me my best chance in life. This chance was possible through adoption.

My biological mother would not let just anyone adopt me. She was Irish, so she wanted someone with an Irish background to adopt me. She was also athletic, a runner, so she wanted someone who was athletic. She had talent in music, so she wanted the people who adopted me to be musical. She wanted an older couple that had been married for a long time. The most important thing she wanted for me was a lifetime in the Catholic faith.

That's when "my parents" came along. My mom and dad had wanted a baby for a long time, but for some reason they just could not have one. Both are active Catholics. My dad was an athletic runner, and my mom is Irish. Everything matched perfectly. My parents are the kind of people my biological mother wanted to raise me. After a long, involved process, I was adopted.

You may wonder what this has to do with God's presence in my life. It has a lot to do with it. God put me with these people. God put me on this track. It's hard being a teenager in the nineties, let alone an adopted teenager. There are so many questions in everyday life that I just can't answer because I'm adopted. I hope that one day I will be able to meet the woman who brought me into the world and ask her all my questions, but for now I will rely on God and my parents to help me through adolescent life. It helps to know that this is the track God put me on, and I must follow it no matter what.

Jaymee Marois
Mount Saint Charles
Academy
Woonsocket, Rhode Island

Basking
in the Warmth

A few months ago, my favorite aunt and uncle separated. The clambake was the last time I saw them before they went their separate ways, and I will always remember the way my uncle was then.

Behind the driveway some men were tending to a huge bonfire that made the trees appear to dance in a sea of smoke and cast writhing shadows on everything. A few feet away, some others were cooking lobster and steak on a barrel grill. The air smelled of burnt seaweed, and I could hear the wood popping and sizzling. Farther on another group of men played horseshoes, drank beer, and filled the night air with their laughter. Most of the women were sitting at picnic tables and under tarps, huddled around insect-repellent candles that glowed softly until little Samantha came along and blew them out. My young cousins were running around everywhere, trying to do everything at once—play volleyball, badminton, football, and roast marshmallows on the various fires.

Wandering under a sky full of lazily floating ash, I found my favorite uncle, Ron. Slightly past middle age, Uncle Ron is the kind of guy who always takes time to listen to me. He is the best company to have. He was wearing a pair of old jeans with a big frayed hole in the back left pocket. I remember teasing him about it. He just smiled that amazing smile. His smoke-stained but otherwise perfect teeth and bright blue eyes made his face so warm and friendly. His eyes could peer right into me, and he would be able to know what I was thinking. No matter what, I couldn't get sick of being around this guy.

While I was talking to Uncle Ron, Aunt Sim, his wife, came over to see how I was doing. She has beautiful chestnut-brown hair that always looks perfect, even under the worst conditions. Her dark brown eyes seemed to capture all color, like two black holes, except they gave off incredible warmth.

Uncle Ron decided that he was going to join the horseshoe tournament, so I got him a beer, sat back, and watched. After it got too dark to play, we stoked up the fire and everyone sat around it. It was cold, so I was wearing Uncle Ron's blue wind-breaker. It smelled just like him, a combination of smoke and cologne. I sat there staring at the fire with Uncle Ron on my left, Aunt Sim behind me, and my cousin Chelsea on my lap. Basking in the warmth, we didn't say much or do much except enjoy one another's company.

While sitting there, a calm peacefulness settled over me. I realize now that that feeling was God's presence. Everybody got along fine, and Uncle Ron and Aunt Sim were happy together. I always get that feeling when I'm near Uncle Ron or when I get mail from him. Now that he and Aunt Sim are separated, it's practically a miracle if I get to see him, so I really treasure my moments with him.

Heather Kennedy
Bishop Grimes High
School
East Syracuse, New York

The Bringer of Light

One of the most important experiences for me in which God was present to help me was the death of my dad. That day in June 1996 was a normal school day and workday. When my dad came home from work, he said his back was hurting. He had a whole bag full of medicine for it. Both my sisters had softball games, and my mom was going to their games, so I was home alone with my dad.

He went up to take a bath and then came downstairs to watch TV. After I finished my homework, I went in to watch with him. I looked over and thought my dad was sleeping, but he wasn't. He had stopped breathing. I went to the phone and dialed 911. The person on the phone wanted me to do C.P.R. on my dad, but I couldn't. I ran over to my neighbor, who is a nurse, to see if she would do C.P.R. on my dad.

She and her daughter came over. The ambulance was on its way. It seemed to take forever for them to come. I didn't stay in the house once the ambulance got there. One of my other neighbors said I should go get my mom and tell her what happened, so I did. By the time we got back, my dad was in the ambulance. My mom got in, too, and went to the hospital.

My sisters and I went over to our neighbors' house. We watched TV, but I was really scared. All I could do now was pray, and that is what I did. After a while the phone rang. It was my mom, telling us we should go home and that she would be back soon. Three of my mom's friends were there cleaning and helping out. I had a feeling that something was wrong right away.

When my mom came home, I think she was literally in shock. I can't imagine the pain she had to go through to tell us that my dad had died. At first, when my mom told us, I was in a different world, as if I was in a bad dream. I was waiting to wake up, but I never did. That painful nightmare was true. My dad, my healthy, happy dad, had died.

Before I went to sleep, I told my mom exactly what had happened when my dad was unconscious. I started to cry and said I was afraid I would fail seventh grade because I had exams the next day. By the time I went to sleep, which was very late, I was glad for my dad that he was in heaven. All through the wake and the funeral, many people tried to comfort us, and we got a lot of cards and letters. Some of my friends visited me, too, but they didn't really know how I felt.

When I went back to school, I didn't have the nicest substitute teacher. He didn't know my dad had died. My mom had called to say I was not to take any tests the first day back. The substitute didn't really care about that, so I just walked out and started to cry. I didn't go back to school again until the last day of school. That was a fun day—my seventh-grade class gave me a yearbook that everyone had signed.

Throughout the summer I didn't feel like I should have fun because my dad wasn't there. By the end of the summer, when I went camping with a friend, I finally felt more normal, like my summer was just beginning. But it was ending. I had no clue what school to go to. My dad had wanted me to go to a Catholic school, so I went to Bishop Ludden, but in late October I transferred to Bishop Grimes, which is closer to home. A lot of my friends from grade school went there, too, so it turned out to be a good decision. Throughout the year, my friends and family helped us all work through our feelings about my dad's death by cooking dinners, watching us, fixing things my dad would have fixed, and just being there to listen.

Now I am in the ninth grade at Bishop Grimes High School. I feel a lot better about my dad's death. My family has made a family even though we are missing Dad. He will always be in our hearts.

On June 27, 1998, my mom will be getting married. Yes, again, to one of the nicest people I have met besides my dad. He lost his wife in a car accident four years ago and was left to raise five children on his own. Through the last year, they have been seeing each other and meeting everyone. My mom is very blessed to have two loves in one lifetime.

I think God was present in all this because I never would have made it without the help of church, the Bible, and God's people, who came to help us. I know life will never be the same, but at least I know God has helped us through this. "God never closes a door without opening a window." This old saying is so true. When something bad happens, God will always be there to bring us light at the end of a dark tunnel.

Amber Rodriguez
Lake Michigan Catholic
High School
Saint Joseph, Michigan

Wishes

When I was in second grade, my parents got divorced. Unlike some children I never thought I was the source of my parents' problems. But I always wondered why God had to do something so horrible to my family. I remember having the feeling that life was a lotto game and God had randomly picked our number. And what a grand prize we had won!

Since I was about eight or nine years old, I have lived with my dad. My mother migrates back and forth between Florida and Indiana. My brother and I spend the weekends with my mom when she is in Indiana.

Both of my parents wanted custody of my brother and me, but since we had recently switched schools and my mom was planning to move, custody was awarded to my dad.

At first everything seemed basically the same; we just didn't get to see my mom as much. Then she was offered a great job in Florida. Since there were no job opportunities for her here, she took it. I cried when she left, but I tried to stay calm. I never wanted my parents to think I was having a hard time dealing with things. I didn't want to cause more problems.

I never really talked to anyone about my parents' divorce or how I felt about it. That's probably why, today, I don't feel comfortable sharing my feelings with anyone, even God.

I think that it was probably for the best that my parents got divorced. They were always fighting. But it caused and is still causing a lot of pain in me. The only thing that I can honestly say I have gained from the divorce is my sense of duty.

As I grew up living with my dad, I took on a lot of responsibility. Nowadays I cook, clean, and do most of the other household chores. Sometimes I get help from my brother. But most of the time, he does things wrong, and I have to do them over again. So I just do them myself.

My friends think that I do too much, and they call me the mother of the house. Taking care of everyone isn't something I choose to do, it's just a part of who I am.

Sometimes I resent having these responsibilities, but I know that things must be done. Even so, sometimes I wish my parents were still together so my load would be lessened. I know it's selfish, but sometimes I wish I were just like every other kid whose parents aren't divorced.

To this day I have never completely dealt with my parents' divorce. I have never had a heart-to-heart talk with either of them about my feelings. I have kept everything to myself, hoping that I could deal with it.

Sometimes I wish that I could have talked to my parents. Or even that I had the courage to do so now. But I don't feel comfortable expressing myself. I wish that God had been a bigger part of my life when I was younger so that maybe I would have someone to talk to now.

Ashley Wiese
Mount Notre Dame
High School
Cincinnati, Ohio

Mothering a Mother

As I went downstairs, I found myself walking through blackness. It was obvious she was still in bed. Usually Mom was up packing our lunches. Not today. Not being able to handle certain things with my dad out of town, she took shelter in her bedroom, along with a beer or two.

Driving home from school that day, I noticed Mom's car was where it had been when we left in the morning, eleven hours ago. I decided to check on her to see what was up. I made my way to her bedroom slowly. Lightly, I pushed the door open and poked my head in. She was sleeping deeply, almost completely hidden by the down comforter. Her hair was matted from being in bed so long. The room was faintly warm and had the aura of a prison cell.

I'd make dinner tonight, but what about the next few days? Was I about to play the role of mother for the week?

Tuesday passed in a similar way, and Wednesday morning I got ready and went straight to the kitchen to pack our lunches. It was becoming routine.

"Meg, we're running out of food. How much money have you got?"

"None. I gave mom the eighty dollars I borrowed on Sunday. That was all I had. I have been looking for her wallet, but I can't find it. Dad said if we needed money to get it from her."

"Brian found it last night in the laundry hamper with a bunch of empty wine bottles. It won't do much good, there's only ten dollars in it," Lynn said.

I went reluctantly back to her room to check on her again. I peeked cautiously around the corner and my nose caught the stench of old air, now thicker with the odor of alcohol. I stood for a minute staring at the lump of comforter, wondering if she was even alive. All at once she flopped over. Her body was limp and heavy, and it seemed to take a great effort just to move. As I began to back out, she opened her swollen eyes, revealing thickly glazed and minutely dilated pupils. Those eyes looked straight into mine without even seeing me. Her gaze was a sharp stab to my heart. There was no motherly affection there, no caring. Then I looked at her glazed eyes and flushed face and saw the alcohol demon inside her. She went to take a step forward, but her alcohol-infested brain decided against it and she staggered, grabbing the bedpost for support. I put out a supportive arm that she grasped tightly. It was more than just physical support. Her eyes welled with tears. I remained emotionless on the outside but melted inside. She did not say a word but just clung to me.

Her state depressed me immensely. She was no longer the mother—I was. I gently guided her back to the shelter of her covers and thought, where is God now?

Lindsay Clampitt
Saint Gertrude
High School
Richmond, Virginia

No More Mothers Cry

I woke up at 5:30 a.m. on January 22, 1998. It was a cold and dreary morning, and I was not fully prepared for the experience ahead. It was one that would shape and change my life.

This was the day that I would embark on a trip to Washington, D.C., to take part in the March for Life Rally. I was extremely excited and anxious about what was to come. At 7:15 I arrived at the Columbian Center. The trip to Washington was being sponsored by the Knights of Columbus. I walked inside to find my friends, who were as excited as I was. We boarded the bus, and I chose a window seat beside my friend Nancy.

While we were on the bus, we did something I will never forget. Blessed rosaries were distributed to everyone, and the whole bus joined in prayer. It was amazing to be surrounded by people you didn't even know, and to all be united as one voice, praying for the exact same cause. At that moment I realized that God was a passenger on the bus with us, residing in each of our hearts. We were there acting as his disciples.

Finally we arrived in Washington. The streets were filled with thousands of people. As soon as I exited the bus, I was approached by a reporter for the Richmond Times-Dispatch. A battery of questions ensued, and my faith was challenged with each one. I answered each and every question confidently, proud to stand up for my beliefs. God's presence allowed me to answer the questions without hesitation. As I spoke I felt that God was speaking through me.

Occasionally, while we made our way through the crowds, I would just look up and smile at someone passing by. I felt like I knew everyone there personally. When we arrived at the Ellipse, I grabbed a sign and ran to catch up with the group. My sign said, "The Natural Choice Is Life!" After we had marked out a territory, we saw some friars and nuns standing nearby. The nuns held their rosaries close to their hearts. I realized that not only was God there in each of us but the church was there, physically showing its support of this cause. Soon after, a Christian music group was broadcast over the loudspeakers. Our group began to dance around and belt out the refrains to the songs. We were simply having a good time.

An elderly Irish woman approached us. She told us, with a tear in her eye, that she had never seen such enthusiasm from today's young women. She told us that we had inspired her. Not only did this make us feel good, it deepened our belief in what we were doing. A little bit later, we began to notice that it was freezing outside. My face, legs, hands, and toes were numb. We decided that our purpose at the rally was more important than our comfort.

Soon the speakers began, and each one discussed the issue from a different perspective, but all were united in the belief that life is sacred. One speaker commented about one of the first signs I saw when we arrived. It read, "No more babies die, no more mothers cry." The speaker indicated that over half of the women suffering from depression in our country have had an abortion. Most women that have an abortion live with a great guilt for the rest of their life: What would their child's future have been like?

While the speakers continued, I looked around at the crowd. I noticed a man in his nineties who was wearing a starched doctor's coat. On the back of the coat, in red felt letters, was the statement, "Forgive me father for I have sinned, I pray for those I taught to save lives, who are now taking them. THIS IS MY PENANCE." The man was a professor of medicine. Some of his students had gone on to open abortion clinics. Upon seeing this man, I could tell that he truly regretted that some of his students had decided to choose such a lifeless career. I also knew that the same God who was with me that day was also with the doctor.

The march was about to begin! I was surrounded by people. Some were even standing in trees, proudly displaying their signs. As we marched, we chanted and sang. Babies, elementary school students, teenagers, and the elderly were all taking part in the march. I knew that God was walking with us, too. Many said that each year they see more and more pro-life teens publicly supporting the cause. I think it's wonderful that other people my age are working together toward a solution that will eventually save lives. The feeling is indescribable.

The law still stands. *Roe v. Wade* has not been overturned. With the assistance of God, I will continue to work for this law to be changed. Hopefully my children will not have to be a part of this rally because the law will by then be nonexistent. The March for Life Rally was rooted in faith and the presence of God. I hope that others can begin to see the true value of life and that one day no more mothers will have to cry.

Emily Bowen
Coyle-Cassidy High School
Taunton, Maryland

Casey Franco
Saint Aloysius
High School
Vicksburg, Mississippi

A Small Act of Giving

This past summer my mom and I spent five days on a mission-ary trip in Saltillo, Mexico. My CYO (Catholic Youth Organiza-tion) went with other CYOs in the Jackson, Mississippi, diocese. The trip was a very special experience for me in several ways, mainly because I was able to help others who truly needed help. The people in Mexico used whatever food you gave them to last them until the next donation, lived in communities where the only available water was stored in dirty barrels, and were con-sidered lucky to have four walls and a roof over their heads. What I witnessed in Saltillo was real, yet it was like nothing I had ever seen before. They made do with the few things they did have: faith in each other and faith in God.

One particular day stands out most in my mind. We were at one of the ranchos, a small community. It was so small that we celebrated Mass on a hilltop, under a large tree, because there was no church nearby. After the Mass was over, we followed our routine and began passing out food, clothes, medicine, makeup, toys, and other donations to the Mexican families.

My mom and I were passing out makeup to the girls. As we were handing out lipstick and fingernail polish, an old woman came up to me and pointed to her eyes. I didn't know Spanish and she didn't know English, so body language was our only means of communication. Right away I looked in my bag of makeup for some eye shadow, but I didn't have any. I looked at the old lady, held up my hands, and shook my head no, hoping that she would understand.

Well, she didn't. She kept pointing to her eyes and pulling on my arm. I called over to Francesco, one of the few translators in our group, and asked him to tell her that I had no eye shadow. He spoke to the old lady and then turned around and told me that she didn't want any makeup. She was blind and wanted a pair of sunglasses because the sun hurt her eyes. But I knew we had no sunglasses in our bags of donations.

My mom had been standing there with me the whole time. Now she looked in her purse and took out her only pair of Oakley-brand sunglasses. She gave them to the old woman. With an enormous smile on her face, the woman put on her new sunglasses, turned to Francesco, and spoke to him in Spanish. He told my mom that she said, "Thank you. I love you very much."

My mom immediately began crying, and we were both overwhelmed with happiness. I believe that through this old woman, Christ was present among us. By this small act of giving, I was rewarded with a greater gift: serving Christ. As the Scriptures read, "Whatsoever you do to the least of my people, that you do unto me."

Daniel M. Benninger
De Smet Jesuit
High School
Saint Louis, Missouri

The Franchise Player

I sat with twenty other teenagers, waiting for a special guest. We had no idea whom it would be. From the hints that our youth minister had given us, most of us were guessing it was some famous sports figure. I thought it might be Ozzie Smith or Mark McGwire. It had to be someone famous, because they kept referring to him as "the franchise player."

Finally it was seven o'clock. Mass was over, but no special guest had arrived. The small house we used for prayer group was clean, our name tags were in place, and everyone was dressed up and on their best behavior, all waiting to hear words of wisdom from some prominent figure. We all mingled for a while discussing our guesses or catching up on what had happened in the past week. A news reporter from the Saint Louis Post Dispatch was interviewing groups of teens, and the anticipation was building. Then our youth minister told us all to move to another room where a number of chairs faced the front.

We sat down, and an unfamiliar man introduced himself. He said that he was with the Saint Louis Cardinals organization. As a member of that organization, this man narrowed down the options for who the franchise player would be. He also made it seem that tonight, for real, one of my sports heroes was going to be standing before me. I began to get very anxious. Then the announcement was made: He was here, so everyone needed to quiet down. This was amazing. Everyone had gone through such physical and mental preparation for this, and now it was all going to pay off.

The lights dimmed and in walked Fr. Mike Butler. But no prominent athlete was with him. Instead he brought with him a monstrance carrying the Body of Christ, Jesus. It was all a bit overwhelming at first, but as I followed Father, others, and Christ into a small chapel room, it started to clear up. The man before me was not any celebrity who signs autographs but the Son of God who has redeemed the world.

I knelt down in adoration and felt immense peace. The troubles and worries of school and home did not exist right now because I was talking to God, who was there to listen, and I was there to praise him. Afterward I tried to imagine what I would have done differently if I had known that we would be experiencing adoration and not a speech by a professional athlete. Would I have come? Would I have prepared as much? As I pondered these thoughts, I realized that they didn't matter at that instant. What mattered was that I was able to leave that night with a greater respect for the physical presence of Christ in the Eucharist and a peace to last me a lifetime.

Angela Elaine Maria Yust
Saint Elizabeth Academy
Saint Louis, Missouri

Always with Me

I was eleven years old. My concept of God was not what it is today. I believed in God but didn't understand why bad things happened to good people. I thought that if something bad happened to me, I must have done something wrong.

My mom died, and all I could do was blame myself. I felt that I was being punished for something I had done, or maybe I didn't deserve such a good mother.

I remember the day of my mother's funeral like it was yesterday. I was overwhelmed with all the sympathy cards, flowers, and casseroles. People who had not shown their faces for years were there acting as if they were very devoted friends and family. I was so furious, I wanted to scream. I had never felt so alone in my life.

A family member told me that I had one week to grieve my mother's death, and then I had to grow up. On the outside I was calm and collected and appeared to be very mature, but on the inside I was crumbling to pieces. "Why me?" was all that kept going through my head.

When I went to church, I felt that the ladies were whispering to one another, "That's the poor little girl that lost her mom." I didn't want people feeling sorry for me. Every time I looked at the altar, all I could remember was my mother's casket lying in front of it. I had gotten to the point where I wouldn't eat, sleep, go to school, or even be with my friends. I just wanted all the pain to go away. My mom was everything to me. I was her only child, and she did everything in the world for me. She was an excellent wife and mother, so dedicated to my dad and me.

It wasn't until Mother's Day that I realized my mother was really gone. My dad missed my mom just as much as I did. He was looking for an explanation, too.

One morning very early, I woke up out of my sleep. I looked at my alarm clock. It was 5:00 a.m. I wasn't due to get up for another two hours. Then I looked toward my door and my mother appeared there. She was beautiful. Her hair was long and her skin was radiant—there was a glow around her whole body. The image came closer and smiled at me. Then she turned around and she was gone.

I thanked God for letting me know my mom was all right. I felt so peaceful. I knew now that she was watching over me.

Later that day I told my dad. He started to cry, and he told me that the night before, in his prayers, he had asked God to give me some sort of sign that my mother was okay. His prayers had been answered.

I knew then that God was working in my life and that there is a reason for everything. I was no longer resentful. I no longer felt that I was being punished. Today I strongly believe that God will give us only what we can handle.

To this day the loss of my mom isn't easy, but it has made me so grateful for the things I do have. My dad and I have become so close through it all. And now I am never alone, because God and Mom are always with me.

Cristina Quintero
Archbishop Curley-Notre
Dame High School
Miami, Florida

Alessandra

It would be very easy to sit here in front of my computer and recall all the times that I have felt God's absence in my life. I remember my grandfather having a stroke, my father kicking me out of the house, my mother moving away, my losing friends and boyfriends. If I had been asked to write this essay a year ago, or even a few months ago, those are just a few of the topics I could have chosen to write about. But I am at a different place in my life right now. I feel freer, and more content to explore the times God has been present in my life.

This makes the task much more difficult. God's presence is so personal and magical that no words in any language could ever describe the experience. I could give someone an idea of the joy, inner peace, and tranquillity that I have felt when God has revealed himself to me through another person, but an idea is not enough. Experiencing God is the pinnacle of any positive moment and the complete converse of every negative one. I have encountered this wonderful Being through my little sister.

When my stepmother first told me the news of her pregnancy, I was excited, anxious, and scared, unsure of what the future was going to hold. The nine months of waiting stimulated an array of emotions in me. The day Alessandra Victoria was born, however, I knew exactly how I felt about her.

Her birth was unforgettable. The first time I saw her, I saw the purest and most innocent form of life I had ever seen. In front of me lay this little creature, completely new and ignorant of the world, completely dependent upon others to live, as we are upon God. I was in heaven at the sight of this purity and perfection, or as close to perfection as one could ever get. This is exactly how God becomes present in my life. Every day with my sister since her birth has been a new and totally different experience. Each time I am with her, I am reminded of God's unconditional love for me, much like Alessandra's love for me now.

I remember one time when she was about five months old. I spent the whole day feeding her, changing her, and just loving her. She held me and slept on me the entire day. Everyone in the family was always preoccupied with entertaining her, and all she needed was love and care. Other times when I am alone with her, she looks at me and I look at her and we understand each other. She can't speak, and I really don't talk to her much. It is just the act of being together that is so beautiful.

Sometimes Alessandra will look at me and start laughing. She laughs a lot and out loud. Sometimes that is the best thing in the world to hear. When I hear her laugh, I begin to realize that she is her own person, not just a little doll, which is how I had previously perceived babies. She is real and human, and not only is she my stepmother's baby and my sister, she is an individual created by God.

This is a wonderful yet scary thought. She will have her own experiences to go through, and that is great. She will also unfortunately have to go through many bad moments and terrible experiences. She will often feel alone, and she will sometimes need to be alone. She will feel God's absence. It is so ironic that the one person who reveals God so fully to me will have difficulty finding him in her life. I guess the truth is that we all have God inside us; we just don't see him all the time. When the time comes, I will help Alessandra, like she helped me, find God in her life.

Brian Weber
Father Judge High School
Philadelphia,
Pennsylvania

Kevin, My Brother

My younger brother, Kevin, is the main example of how I feel God's presence in my life. There are others way, too, but Kevin is the strongest.

When I was very young, about three years old, something happened that changed my life. One summer day Kevin and I were playing. My mom decided to put my brother down for a nap. Then I went downstairs with my mom to do the wash. Suddenly we heard a crash.

We went upstairs to check on my brother, but he wasn't there. What happened isn't clear. All I remember is running downstairs and seeing my brother lying on the floor in the dining room. Under his head was a towel, and there was blood all over it.

The paramedics came and quickly took my brother away. I found out later that Kevin had apparently pushed the screen out of the bedroom window and fallen about twelve feet. During the fall he had hit his head on the air conditioner.

I think I was in a state of shock after that. The doctors said they didn't know if he would make it. My mom and I prayed day and night. The doctors finally told us that Kevin would survive, but he would be paralyzed for life.

We thought our prayers had been answered, but to think that Kevin might never be able to walk or use his hands again was horrible. I kept offering my prayers up to God, because I wanted to be able to hang out and play with my brother as a normal person again.

Throughout the next few years, Kevin needed to go through more surgeries and physical therapy. The doctors had to put a plate in his head so the injured area would always be protected. Before the plate was put in, he had to wear a helmet for protection. The injury also affected his vision and his ability to read.

My prayers seemed to be almost completely answered when the doctors said Kevin would be paralyzed on just one side of his body. By this time I was just happy to have my brother alive. I didn't care anymore if he could walk.

What happened next was amazing. With therapy and hard work, Kevin learned to walk. It hardly matters that he has a limp. And he not only regained the ability to walk—he could also ride a bike and wrestle with me.

I am extremely proud of Kevin for going to therapy and working so hard to get as far as he has. He recently graduated from Saint Timothy's grade school, where he was in special education, and he is now a freshman at Archbishop Ryan High School. Although he is still partially paralyzed in his right arm and leg, he doesn't give up. He has faced much adversity and has won. With God's presence my brother survived a nearly fatal accident and is alive and doing well.

Sarah Pulsifer
Coyle-Cassidy High School
Taunton, Maryland

Megan Jefferies
Kennedy-Kenrick Catholic
High School
Norristown, Pennsylvania

Guidance and Responsibility

I have attended Catholic schools all my life, and that is where I found my profound love for God. It was in school that I learned the meaning of God's holy presence in my life and the importance of God in helping me live my life to the fullest.

I have experienced all the normal aspects of being a teenager—school, friends, problems, curfews. Of course I go through all these daily challenges like most of my peers, but now I have one more challenge to add to the list—responsibility.

After three years of assisting in CCD classes at my parish, I was asked to become a teacher. I really did not know how to respond. I loved assisting at CCD, but I wasn't sure that I was ready and willing to take the next step, which included sacrificing a lot of my time. I also wasn't sure if I would be able to handle the responsibility. I thought about it for a while and then asked for advice from friends, teachers, and my parents, all of whom said it was "up to me." Then I prayed to God. Now understand, I believe in God Almighty. I believe God is present among us always. I know he is always there to listen to us, but I was always a little unsure of the idea of actually receiving an "answer." To me prayer was like having a conversation with one of the quietest people on earth, as if I were talking to myself. Nonetheless I prayed for guidance and reassurance, which I feel is all you can truly pray for. I don't think people, even the most holy, pray to God and wait for a response "out loud."

Time went on, and I reached the point where I had to either accept this new responsibility or decline out of fear. I decided to go for it and accept the offer to take on this most honored and prestigious role in the lives of God's children.

I teach a second-grade class consisting of eight children. I teach them about Jesus, the Lord our Savior, and try to answer their tough questions with all the love, respect, and knowledge I have. I still have plenty of questions myself, but I keep them to myself, for I know one day the answers will be revealed to me.

The children are so innocent, not aware of all the temptations and pressures that await them in life. They come to class ready (most of the time) to participate and learn about Jesus Christ.

I can't imagine my life without them. It is only once a week, yet I have grown with them in faith and knowledge. It may only be a very small contribution to spreading the word of God, but to me it is tremendous.

The impact and holy presence of God has inspired me to live my faith daily and to help these children experience the love and joy I have been shown. I feel proud to be able to have the light of God shine through me for all the world to see.

Erin Keegan
Mount Notre Dame
High School
Cincinnati, Ohio

Checking In

During my junior year of high school, I worked at an Italian restaurant called Mancino's Pizzas and Grinders. It is a small restaurant, and mostly high school kids work there.

One cold November evening, I was asked to make a delivery to a house not far from the store. We were not very busy, so I said I'd do it. The order was for a party, so it was sort of large, consisting of a few pizzas and many sandwiches called grinders. I'd probably get a good tip, so that was another reason to go.

As soon as the order was ready and packed up, I left to make the delivery. When I got to the house, I went to the front door with the two delivery bags and rang the bell. They invited me to step inside because it was so cold outside, and I started to hand the food to the man and the woman. I had given them all the pizzas and had started pulling out the grinders when a side order of pizza sauce fell out of the bag. It spilled all over their white carpet.

I offered to clean up the mess and give them the order for free. By doing that, it meant the money would come out of my pocket, which bothered me a little, but it was my fault anyway. The family told me not to worry about cleaning up the pizza sauce—things like that happen to everyone, they said. They handed me a check and said to keep the change. I told them their order was free, but they insisted on paying me, and gave me a tip, even though I didn't think I deserved one.

Driving back to Mancino's, I was really upset. I got inside the store and told everyone what had happened. They told me it's over, not to worry, and to just put the check in the cash register. But when I reached into my pocket, the check was gone!

By this time I couldn't believe all that had happened to me on this one delivery. Everyone searched my car and looked around the back parking lot, but the check was nowhere to be found. We all returned to our work. Then I decided to go outside one more time and look around for the check, because I really didn't want the money to come out of my own pocket. As I walked around the parking lot with tears coming down my cheeks, the check just blew right over my feet.

I was so happy and relieved. I felt that this was God's way of letting me know that everything was going to be all right. I felt God was with me throughout the whole experience—the family had been so understanding about the accident, and then I found the check. I went back inside Mancino's and told everyone I had found the check, and then I just sat down and thanked God and my dad in heaven for being with me and watching over me through it all.

Jacob Giordano
Bishop Grimes High
School
East Syracuse, New York

Blessed Tears

Many people say that they have close encounters with angels, Mary, Jesus, and even God. I would like to tell a story about a time when God was profoundly present in my life.

This story took place on the birthday of the Most Holy Virgin Mary. My fifth-grade class at Saint John the Baptist Academy went to the church next door to pray, offer homage, and give flowers to Mary. With religion books in hand, we all sat down in the pews in front of a statue of Mary and the baby Jesus. While reading a prayer out of our religion books, I felt special, as if I was part of something bigger. But I didn't want to show what I was feeling, because even in a Catholic school, showing how religious you are or how much you enjoy prayer just isn't cool.

We continued with our little birthday party, so to speak, saying prayers, offering homage, and talking personally with Mary. One on one. Just ourselves and Mary. I don't know if I can speak for the whole class, but I actually enjoyed it. No matter how stupid or uncool it sounds, I really felt joy deep down, even if I didn't show it. We each brought a flower to the statue, but it was something more than just a flower. It was a personal gift from us, to the mother of our Savior.

After bringing up our gifts, the ceremony was almost over. All those who wished to say additional prayers at the foot of the statue were welcome to, and all those who were ready to go were welcome to leave. I stayed and continued to pray along with some classmates. Our teacher, Mrs. Lippoldt, a tremendously spiritual, faithful, kind, and gentle woman, left with the children who wanted to leave so that she could keep an eye on them. The rest of us eventually finished praying and were ready to leave and join up with our classmates. But for some reason we were compelled to take a last look at the statue. As we looked we noticed that the statue had begun to cry!

We ran over to it to make sure we weren't seeing things. The statue was surely crying! Some of us were in tears, others in shock, but we all ran out to get our teacher and the rest of the kids to share in this extraordinary experience. The small class crowded around to see the tears. I lay down prostrate on the floor, for I felt, and still feel, that I was not worthy to have seen this or even to be in the presence of such a miracle. Even face down on the floor, in the most humble of positions, I still felt disrespectful.

We all laughed when a classmate almost tripped over me, but we then went back to the state of shock. Still shaken up, we walked back to the classroom like a crowd of zombies. We got into the room with just enough time to talk about it before the bell rang for school to end. When most of the class had gone, those of us remaining looked up at the picture of the Sacred Heart our beloved teacher kept above the blackboard. The picture began to glow. Afraid and amazed, we again ran out of the classroom and shared this experience with our teacher, class, and parents.

This was a very powerful, beautiful, and meaningful experience for me. It helped me to realize that God really loves us and is always present in our lives, even when we don't know it.

Adam Law
Peninsula Catholic
High School
Newport News, Virginia

My Father's Hand

About a month ago, something happened to me that I will probably not forget for a long time. My dad, a lieutenant colonel in the Air Force, was assigned to Korea, and he has to stay there for a year.

I will never forget the day we saw him off. The ride to the airport was very quiet. We were all so downhearted. I do not know what the others were thinking, but I was remembering some of the good times I had spent with my dad in the past weeks. Most of all I was thinking about the trip my family had just taken to Florida. I had the time of my life there! I think my father and the rest of the family did, too. But like all good times, it came to an end.

When we finally arrived at the airport, my brothers and I grabbed my father's luggage and went through the entrance with my father and mother. We checked his luggage in and headed to the departure gates. We sat there and started to talk. We talked about what we will do when he returns this summer. We talked most of all, though, about how much we were going to miss one another.

When it came close to the time when he needed to board the plane, the whole family was very unhappy. We all got teary as he started walking into the plane. I think at that moment I had mixed feelings. I was sad for myself, but I felt even more sad for my father. After all, when he left we could all comfort one another, but he would not have anybody. He would be alone. I think he had the hardest time saying good-bye of any of us. Right before my father left though, I distinctly remember him saying, "Don't forget to go to church."

My emotions that day were very strong. I was sad, but more than anything, I think I was mad. I asked myself the question that everybody must ask at least three hundred times in their life, "Why me?" At that moment I was angry with God for letting this happen to my family. At the airport I felt no hope or comfort. I felt lost and empty. I felt that God was absent.

Over the next few days, I was in a really bad humor. I did not feel like doing anything. And although at the time he said them, my father's parting words did not mean anything to me, I felt him holding my hand and pulling me to church the next Saturday. It felt very strange. At church I could not stop thinking about my father and the good times we'd had before he left. The feeling of emptiness was returning. At that split second though, I also began to feel a little bit of comfort. I realized that I was lucky that my father was only going to be gone for a year. I know that some teenagers do not have fathers. Some teenagers actually go through life not knowing their own father because either he has died or he is living someplace else. I knew that it was going to work out okay in the end.

While these new thoughts raced through my mind, I felt God's presence flowing through me. I felt that God was lead-ing me. Although my father will be gone for the next eleven months, I think that everything will be fine. Almost all my teachers have told me that God works in mysterious ways. I never really thought about it until now. I think a lot of times, we never really think about things such as this until we are made to. Although I miss my father very much, I realize now that God is there for me and always will be.

J. A. M.
John F. Kennedy Memorial
High School
Burien, Washington

My Heart

It's not that I don't believe in God, I do. I was baptized when I was a baby, so I did not have much choice. Ever since elementary school, I've had engraved in my head every single passage, prayer, and religious belief that the Bible or the church has to offer. I've recited these things and believed that God existed, but I did not feel God's presence. For me it was like it was in the Bible—God was there for some people, while turning his light and warmth away from others who had failed to be his people. Somewhere along the line, I knew I had screwed up, because I did not feel God's light or warmth. So along with going to church on Sundays, I started to go with my mom to a Mother Perpetual vigil that was held on Tuesdays. We'd kneel and recite a ten-minute prayer for the hopeless and the lowly, then be blessed by the priest. I must have been blessed fifty times with water, but I didn't feel blessed. The harder I sought God, it seemed, the more I remained in the darkness.

Besides being a spiritually messed-up person, I'm not a very strong person. I admit I cry easily, and little things get me down. I think it's easier to love others than it is to love yourself. I could care less what happens to me as long as I can protect others. Yet when the people I love the most struggle and get hurt, I am very vulnerable. Especially when it's the strongest person in my life—to watch her endure so much pain almost tore me apart.

One Tuesday at school, I was told I had a "family emergency." Being a natural pessimist, I imagined the worst. While everyone was at lunch, I wandered the empty hallways, trying to decide what it could have been. The forty-five-minute wait was a lifetime. My dad and younger sister arrived, looking very somber. My dad was smiling and joking as he drove, but his nervous and quick actions told me something was very wrong. I kept asking what it was, even though I didn't want to hear. Finally my sister told me, "Mom had a heart attack." The very words sent a sharp pain through my stomach. After that nobody said anything. I took my seat belt off and laid down in the back, crying to myself.

I stayed like that until we reached the hospital. I ran ahead even though I didn't know where I was going. Mom was in surgery, and there was nothing we could do but wait. It must have been four hours or more before we heard anything. At last we were able to see her. I tried to hold back tears as I looked on the sight of the one who held and carried me when I felt powerless, now hooked up to machines, powerless. After less than five minutes, I couldn't stand it anymore. I took off running. I felt sick, like fainting. The one whom I loved and admired with all my heart—in a way my mother was my "heart"—with her unconditional love, her actions, her support, and her guidance, she kept me "alive." As I was imagining the death of my heart, my brother caught up with me. I saw that I wasn't alone, that my sisters and brother were also feeling the same way. The four of us huddled together. It was the first time that all of us were serious. It almost scared me. I looked at my younger sister. She didn't cry, not once. I envied her strength. I wished I could stay strong like that, instead of falling apart like I was.

When they went home, I stayed at the hospital. I had to be near, just in case something bad might happen, though I knew I wouldn't be able to do much. It was impossible to sleep. The noises from the machines and all-out fear kept me from closing my eyes. Late at night I heard the cries of another patient who had also had a heart attack. He kept yelling, "Oh God! Kill me now! It hurts—it hurts! Nurse, give me a gun so that I can shoot myself! Oh God!" These haunting words continued throughout the whole night, and still today they echo in my mind. He was alone; there was no one in that room with him to calm or comfort him. I found myself relating to him. That same hurt, yet in a different form, was a weight in my chest.

Then, between sobs, that other patient started to pray— prayers that I had known by heart for years. I started to whisper the prayers. Before, these prayers had been just words, but at that moment, they were the only comfort I could find. At that moment, as I prayed, I wasn't looking for any response. I just wanted to remove the pain from my heart. Then everything else went silent. All I could hear was my own voice, whispering in the night. I was relieved just to let it all out, and perhaps some-one was listening. I don't know. But at that moment, I felt com-forted and almost weightless.

As days passed and my "heart" recovered, my mom told me that I was now her strength. I couldn't believe that anybody would say that, but I realized I wasn't in it alone. All along God was with me in the darkness, pulling me through hard times, even though I tried to break myself away. Maybe God lets bad things happen so people can grow closer together, for that's what happened to my family and friends. I've learned to hope. I've learned the real meaning of prayer. Though I don't consider myself to have a big heart, big enough to love everyone and myself at the same time, I have to admit that I am stronger.

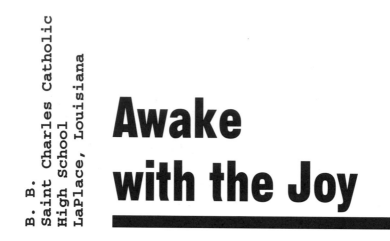

B. B.
Saint Charles Catholic
High School
LaPlace, Louisiana

Awake with the Joy

We all woke up that morning at 5:30 because we were so eager to begin Christmas day. We ran into the living room, and our eyes were glued to all the colorfully wrapped presents stacked under the tree. My dad lit up the tree, and the colors illuminated the green pine tree standing tall in our living room. The smell from the pine tree and the taste of hot chocolate and marshmallows hit my nose and my tongue and made me feel warm and satisfied. We tore open the presents, and you could hear many squeals of delight coming from our home. I gave my mom, dad, and sisters their presents and watched their faces light up with joy as they opened them.

After opening all our presents, we were awake with the joy of the holiday. We packed up the car to take presents to my grandparents and cousins. We arrived at the house and gave hugs and Merry Christmas greetings all around. We walked into the living room and couldn't believe our eyes when we saw all the presents under the tree. The kids could hardly wait to get started. After all the presents had been opened, we went into the dining room to have a great Christmas feast. When we all got so full we couldn't eat anymore, we thanked everyone for our great Christmas and got ready to go home.

When we got home, we loaded the car with still more presents for my other grandparents, Grandmom and Granddad. This was going to be a great Christmas because my cousins,

Mamaw, and my aunts and uncles would be there for the holidays. We arrived at the house and were greeted by more warm holiday wishes, along with the familiar sounds of a holiday football game. All the kids went into the house and were soon busy handing out and unwrapping gifts. Then we all went to a restaurant where we had the most wonderful time. We all ate and ate and ate. We had so much fun and laughed and enjoyed ourselves the whole time. This time was especially special to me because it turned out to be the last Christmas I would spend with my great-grandmother, Mamaw. She passed away since then, and having those wonderful, warm memories of her really made her loss easier for us to accept.

That evening back at Grandmom's, I fell asleep because I was so tired from all the excitement of this great day that God had blessed me with. I woke up a while later, and everyone was watching *Star Wars*. Then the kids started a popcorn fight, and soon we had popcorn kernels all over the floor. I went home that night with my heart and soul fully warmed with God's magical gift: the gift of love and family.

Although to some people this may not seem like an important experience of God's presence, for me it was important and heartwarming. I had the warmth and love of my family around me and the aura of God's presence swirled everywhere among us.

Dennis A. Carbone
Bishop Grimes High School
East Syracuse, New York

Glowing Embers

For the past few years, I have felt the presence of God in my life. Just this past summer, though, I felt God full strength.

For a week and a half of the summer, I went to Virginia for a family trip with my father, my stepmother, Dawn, and my four-year-old sister, Danielle. From the start, my father and I never really got along well. We always argue about this or that, and my dad just loves to argue. This vacation would be no exception.

On the day we arrived, it was stifling hot, and setting up camp became a real chore. Soon I saw the pattern develop, little by little: we were really starting to get on one another's nerves. Throughout the entire trip, we always seemed to be occupying each other's space. By the end of the trip, it was apparent how very distant and different my father and I were from each other.

On the way home, we cut our drive in half by staying in New Jersey for the night. While setting up camp there, my father and Dawn had a little fight, and Dawn kind of cut herself off from the rest of us for the night by staying in the trailer. Somehow I was dragged into the whole thing, and my father didn't want to speak to me either.

When it started to get dark, my father told me to gather some kindling for a fire. I did, and he began to light it. For some reason the kindling just burned away and the fire did not catch. I gathered more and we tried again, to no avail. He told me that this was the last time. I knew that if this didn't work, the night would end and we would go to sleep unresolved. While I gathered some more kindling, I whispered a short prayer that God would send the Holy Spirit to make this fire blaze.

My dad tried again. All we got were glowing embers. Thinking of my prayer, I ever-so-gently (my dad looked at me like I was dumb) blew into the embers. To our amazement the fire caught, and within minutes we had a roaring conflagration. I thanked God silently for this and told my dad that this was our "miraculous fire." I think he knew in his heart who had done it.

For a couple of minutes, we sat and stared at our miracle, and soon my dad turned and said, "Let's throw some wood on this fire to keep it going and go for a little walk." Our little walk turned into a pretty long one, and we talked about a lot. That night I felt closer to my father than I have ever felt before.

While we were walking, we bought some Jiffy Pop to roast over our fire. We settled back at the camp, and I watched my father as he ridiculously tried to make Jiffy Pop over a fire so large. It worked, and we ate together while we shared more conversation. Soon though I grew tired and decided to go to sleep.

As I drew my covers over me, I said my nighttime prayers. I made sure to thank God for the fire, but then I realized that the fire wasn't the only miracle. That was just the prologue. The bigger miracle was how the Holy Spirit had bonded my father and me that night. I thanked God once again, and my thoughts drifted to my dad, still out by the fire. I knew that he was doing the same thing.

Of course my father and I still have the normal small quarrels that all parents and their children have, but now there is something new. Now we can always talk them out together because we have opened up to each other. God knew that this would happen, and that is why he chose to be present so much more that day. God increased the amount of communication between my father and me tenfold. By this experience I learned that as long as you invite God into all situations, in the end you will have a greater sense that something good was accomplished. Thank you, Father!

Mike McGlothlen
Saint Xavier
High School
Louisville, Kentucky

Michaela
Saint Mark's High School
Wilmington, Delaware

A Good Hold on God

My name is Michaela. I'm going to tell you the story of how I finally saw God in my heart, mind, and life. I never took God that seriously while I was growing up. I did what most kids I knew did—I went to church and prayed that the Mass would end soon. I used to check my watch about every five minutes, impatiently waiting for the priest to finish his talk. I believe that I first saw God in 1996, when my parents got divorced.

I was twelve years old when it happened. My parents had been separated for a couple of months. They had been separated once before, when I was about seven years old, but I knew that this separation was not going to end.

During their first separation, I didn't really understand what was going on around me. I saw my mom getting really sad and my brother not saying or doing anything that even hinted that something was wrong. I had many of my meals at my neighbor's house, because my mother couldn't get out of bed because she was so depressed. I was feeling very confused and hurt. When you're seven years old and in this situation, you basically have nowhere to go. For me God wasn't someone to turn to then. My father returned after a couple of months, and our life as an intact family seemed to continue. That's the background to my story. Now let me tell you about the event that changed my life.

The year was 1996; I was twelve years old. I had grown up to be rather mature for my age. My parents had separated again, and this time I knew what was happening! I still went out with my father every weekend, along with my brother. In my mind I constantly questioned what I was doing there with my father. I came home once to see my mom crying on the couch. She had me sit down with her. She then told me that she and my father were getting a divorce.

At that moment my life became very challenging. I had to make choices that would either ruin my life or make it better. I still never thought to ask God for help. For a couple of months after my parents' divorce, I still would go see my father. But it wouldn't stay that way for long. My last visit with my father was in 1996. He took my brother and me to a Tai Chi picnic. I have never been interested in Tai Chi, but I sat there the whole time watching him doing his Tai Chi with his friend. When I got home that night, I decided that I was no longer the loyal daughter that everyone thought I should be. Since then I haven't talked to him willingly. I had no respect for him as a human, nor did I think it was mentally healthy for me to spend time with someone who couldn't accept the blame for anything. Another reason why I couldn't be loyal to him is that he was disloyal to my mother; he cheated on her.

During the year and a half after the divorce, I didn't believe God was real. I thought God was just some story people made up so they could hope for survival. But I had no hope. I dressed in black, and I remained distant from many people. I didn't really know why I was living. Instead of being my usual open self, I pulled myself farther from people and God. I spent many lunches at my school alone in some corner of the room listening to very dark music. I guess the reason I cut myself off was that I felt if I didn't get attached to anyone, then I couldn't get hurt by anyone. I felt very alone and hurt during this time. I thought that I could not trust anyone, not even God

After two years of being a loner, I finally decided that my life wasn't as bad as I thought it was. I realized that there are a billion other people out there who have been beaten and hurt a lot more than I ever would be. I knew someone who actually had real reasons to be depressed, and that made me think about my life all the more. I started to dress in happier-looking clothes and stopped wearing black lipstick. I decided that I was wasting my life away by being sad. I started to see past all my misfortunes and to see the happiness that was all around me. Now I'm basically like any teenager. I have become more friendly, and I have friends everywhere I go. I have a good hold on life and on God, and I'm not letting go.

I'm now in Saint Mark's High School. Being there has helped, too. I'm a freshman, and I have found my belief in God. I now realize that no matter how hard I try to turn away, God will always be there waiting for me to come back.

Erika L.
Archbishop Curley–Notre
Dame High School
Miami, Florida

Abandoned by God

About two months ago, Valerie called, just as she does every night. My aunt had answered the call, given an exasperated look, and passed me the phone.

"She's been drinking again," my aunt said in Spanish. Unfortunately this came to me as no surprise. But when I started talking to Valerie, I realized that she didn't sound drunk at all. Instead she sounded terribly upset.

"Could you please tell her to stop accusing me of being drunk all the time," Valerie said, her voice breaking. "It's Joey— he's in the hospital—he tried to—commit suicide—"

I cannot begin to explain what I felt at that moment, what I was thinking, or if I was even thinking at all. I was trembling so hard that I could hardly hold the phone. I wanted to sit down, not realizing that I already was. I felt like screaming, but no sound came out. I just listened to Valerie as she told me everything, and waited patiently for her to continue when she would begin to cry.

"Joey bet a lot of money on this football game. When I came home from work, I saw that he had been drinking a lot. I didn't want to stay up and see that our team had lost, so I went to bed. The next morning I went to get the newspaper and saw that his car was still in the driveway. I looked around the house, and then I found him on the floor in another room. His eyes were rolled up into his head—I was—so scared. He must have fallen on his arm because it was three times its normal size. And then I saw the empty bottle of sleeping pills next to him—"

It was like a nightmare. Her words reached me slowly, and she sounded as if she were far away. Joey had tried to kill himself because of money that he had lost? The first thing I thought was that he never would have done this if he had been sober.

The next day I went to see Joey. I was scared. I didn't want to see him in such a serious condition. What if I started to cry? I don't like to cry in front of people. As soon as I saw him, my heart went out to him. The room started spinning and I had trouble breathing. I had to sit down and take a couple of deep breaths to keep from fainting. As much as I tried to stop it, tears started rolling down my face. But what had I expected? We're almost like family.

I've known Valerie and Joey since I was born. My family has known them longer. Both Joey and Valerie are alcoholics. Joey has been drinking since he was a teenager. His grandmother would give him hard liquor when he was a child so that he would go to sleep at night, even though she knew that the disease ran in the family. He throws up in the morning until he has a drink. He's been put in a rehabilitation center three times, but he always goes back to drinking. Valerie is not as bad. She started drinking heavily about three years ago.

I've been praying for Joey for as long as I can remember. He's such a beautiful person. His only flaw is his disease. I keep asking myself what I can do to help. But there is nothing I can do. Only he can help himself, with God's help. I have no more tears left for him.

After Joey was strong enough to talk, psychiatrists went to his room to ask him about that night. He doesn't remember much. But suicide was not his intention at all. The alcohol wasn't giving him that "high" feeling anymore. So he drank the sleeping pills.

The alcohol has badly damaged his liver and he has a form of hepatitis. The doctors say that if he stops drinking for good, he will live to be an old man. But if not, he will die in two years.

In a way I was thankful for that night. I thought, "Joey can get better now. He will stop drinking for good." When he got out of the hospital, it took him a while to regain his strength. He wasn't drinking and he was eating. Valerie wasn't drinking either. I could finally go to their house without having to worry about experiencing that stabbing feeling in my heart.

And then it happened. I was talking to Valerie one night and I heard Joey gagging in the background. I didn't want to believe it. But when I went to their house that weekend, I saw that it was true. They both had started drinking again. And I asked myself, "Why has God abandoned them? Why won't he listen to my prayers?"

The Trouble These Eyes Have Seen

Maria Tilly
Saint Agnes Academy
Memphis, Tennessee

J. E. P.
Central Catholic
High School
Reading, Pennsylvania

New Perspectives

For years I never knew God. It's not that I did not believe in God, I just didn't actually take the time to think of God as something that was real, or as something that had a presence in my life.

Then I read this novel, *The Color Purple*, by Alice Walker. It totally changed my view of God. In one part, two women, Celie and Shug, are talking. Celie asks what God looks like, and Shug answers:

> Don't look like nothing. . . . It ain't a picture show. It ain't something you can look at apart from anything else, including yourself. I believe God is everything. . . .
>
> Listen, God love everything you love—and a mess of stuff you don't. But more than anything else, God love admiration.
>
> . . . I think it pisses God off if you walk by the color purple in a field somewhere and don't notice it. . . . People think pleasing God is all God care about. But any fool living in the world can see it always trying to please us back.

If I try to recall moments of God's presence in my life, there is one that especially sticks out in my mind. During this time in my life, I was very depressed and felt very empty, like there was no point to my life. It was night, and I was riding in a car up

Walnut Street when out of the sky came a big, fiery, lit-up cross. Chills ran up my spine, and at that moment I felt the presence of God. The cross was not an apparition but merely the cross on top of Saint Joseph's Hospital, but I was immediately filled with a sense of well-being. This was the sign I had been waiting for. My feelings of desperation were gone, and I was filled with energy and life.

I also have a faint memory of another incident where I felt God's presence in my life. I was young, probably about nine or ten, and I was paging through a *National Geographic* or some magazine like that, and it had pictures of a war-torn city. I think it was somewhere in Russia, and there was a picture of a statue that had been somewhere outside, in a park or a garden. It was a statue of Jesus with his arms outstretched, but his hands had broken off, perhaps during the war. On the base of the statue someone had written, "Now you must be my hands." It was a profound moment for a simpleminded ten-year-old, because I realized my responsibility as a Christian: to represent Jesus.

I have also felt the absence of God in my life, like when I see the pain and suffering this world can bring and just cannot understand it. How can a loving and merciful God allow so much suffering in the world he created? But I have also found that when you doubt your beliefs, you will soon be given an answer or some way of understanding. So it is good to question what we believe because it gives us new perspectives and shows us new ways of thinking about things.

Michelle Schaeffer
Stella Maris High School
Rockaway, New York

The Way to Go

Once I had a friend named David. He was my closest male friend. David was popular, smart, and very talented. He was almost perfect in the eyes of his parents and his teachers. But under that disguise, he had a serious problem—drug abuse. Only his friends knew of this. After a while he got really desperate for drugs, so much so that he stole from his parents and begged his friends to support his habit. His other friends supported his habit, so I did not approve of them too much. But David and I were still friends.

Some time passed and we drifted apart, but we still kept in touch with each other once in a while. One night he asked me to go to a party with him. It was bad enough that I didn't like David's friends and his habits, but now he wanted me to go to a party with him. Well, I went to appease him. The party lasted only a couple of hours, but I was ready to leave early. There was an uneasy feeling around that place. Most of the people were smoking pot and injecting themselves with drugs. It was really scary watching a guy I had known almost all my life doing things just to fit in.

So I decided to leave the party early. Everyone there was too wasted to drive me home, so I took the bus. I thought David would get home all right. The next day David wasn't in school. I got a little worried, but decided he was probably just too stoned to get out of bed. After school I called him to see

106

what was going on. His father answered the phone, and when he started to speak, I heard the pain in his voice. He told me that David was in the hospital and his mother was there with him.

His father told me what had happened. David and the friends that took him home were in a serious car accident. All the people in the car were either in critical condition or dead. When I heard that, I was really scared. I rushed to the hospital and went near his room. I was nervous about going in, and it took all my courage to do so. I was shocked at what I saw. David's mother told me he would be paralyzed from the chest down. My heart sank into my stomach, and I started to cry.

From that day on, I prayed day and night for David to get better. I prayed, too, that I would be there to comfort him. My best friend is now stuck in a wheelchair for the rest of his life, all because of his addiction. I couldn't explain to myself why the great and powerful God that everyone has faith in couldn't help my friend to understand his mistake. Why couldn't God the "healer" help the only one I loved? Most nights I cried myself to sleep asking, "Why, God, why?" I missed my friend and all our fun.

This was a hard experience for me, but it did show me God's presence in my life. My friend is still alive, and I didn't follow his mistakes. Now David has found God in his life and so have I. We will never lose faith or hope again. And I am grateful that the one true God has shown me the way to go in life.

Manpreet Sidhu
Mount Saint Charles
Academy
Woonsocket, Rhode Island

Answered Prayers

It was late September of 1992, and the summer air still stirred every now and then. I remember the drive from New Jersey back to Boston, two days after my grandmother's death. It all happened so suddenly, but at the time it seemed like a never ending nightmare.

I did not understand what was happening. All I knew was that my mother was not well. My mom gave us all a fright. She had not had a wink of sleep in over a week. No one really knew what was going on in her mind. I guess with the state of depression everyone suddenly fell into, and the loss of her mother, she just could not cope with everything that had happened so suddenly, and she snapped. She did not know where she was or who she was or who her family was.

Some nights I would lie awake listening to her cries and weeping while my father did his best to comfort her. She seemed to be trapped in a far-off world, and no one could reach her. No one could bring her back to us.

I remember one day I was getting ready for school, and she tiptoed down the stairs as if someone were following her. She came over to me. At first she just stood next to me as still as a statue. Then, when I put on my coat and started to walk away, she grabbed me and held onto me with every last bit of strength in her frail, weak body.

Out came a soft, timid voice saying, "Don't leave! You can't leave! When you leave you never come back, you never come back!"

I couldn't say anything. Tears rolled off my terrified face. My aunt came over to us and slowly peeled my mother's arms away from me, like unwrapping a shawl from a newborn.

My aunt said calmly, "Manpreet, don't listen to your mom right now. She doesn't know what she's saying or what she's doing. You get to school and have a good day." Then she took my mom upstairs.

After that day reality struck me in the face like a rude awakening from a pleasant sleep. Sometimes Mom would scare me by constantly shaking when she did not know how to release her anger in any other way, or when she did not know who I was. I would say to her, "Mom, my name is Manpreet, my name is Manpreet!"

She would get upset very quickly with me for thinking she did not know her own daughter. She would tell me, "I know who you are. You're my daughter, you think I don't know who my own daughter is." Every night I would cry myself to sleep, not knowing if my mother would survive another day. I felt all alone in the world, as if no one cared for me, no one heard my cries, no one listened to my sorrows, and no one paid attention to my feelings. One night I stopped myself from crying and walked slowly to my bedroom window. I gazed out at the stars, took a deep breath, and said over and over: "God, if you're listening to me, please, please, all I want in the whole world is for my mom to know who I am and to get better. Please, please help her. I beg you to help her!"

The next morning my aunt found me curled up like a kitten next to the fireplace. Later that day I came from school, and my mom was outside, talking with my aunt. I stepped out of the car, thinking, Just be strong, she'll get better soon.

As I turned around, my mom said to me, "Manpreet, how was your day?"

I ran over to her and hugged her so tight I cannot remember ever letting go of her. At that moment I knew that God had answered my prayers. He had brought my mom back to me, to my family, and to the world.

I pray every night to God, thanking him for bringing my mother back to me. She has no recollection other than the stories we tell her of this trauma in her life, but some things are better left unsaid.

Lauren Zwicky
Immaculate Heart Academy
Westwood, New Jersey

The Blue Candle

I walked silently down the stark white corridor, bravely trying to hold back my tears. I was overwhelmed by the sickening smells of the hospital, by the cries of the patients and the rushing of the doctors. My father and I stepped out of the elevator and into the Coronary Intensive Care Unit. We entered a large room filled with patients recovering from heart surgery. I searched desperately for that familiar face, that familiar voice I could hear in my head. But my comforting mental picture was shattered as a nurse guided us toward a bed in the corner.

"Here is your mom." I barely heard the nurse's words as I stared down at the stranger before me. Covered in tubes and supported by a respirator, it was impossible to believe this was my mother, the same person who this very morning had looked so healthy and optimistic. Tears streamed down my face as I remembered her last words before leaving for surgery: "Don't worry, sweetie. I'm going to be okay." My mom looked so sick; her sallow face seemed distorted, her body enveloped by a huge white sheet. I wanted more than anything to climb into her bed, to have her wake up and comfort me, and give me a huge hug. Instead I stood next to her bed feeling more abandoned and helpless than I had ever felt in my life.

What if my mom was wrong? I thought. What if she's not going to be okay? Is she going to die? These thoughts sent chills down my spine. I had never been more afraid in my life. My father and my aunt tried to comfort me, but I felt as if I were in another world, isolated from any sense of reality.

I left the hospital and walked back to the hotel, oblivious to the commotion around me. I entered my room and threw myself down on the bed, sobbing uncontrollably. Why was this happening to me? Why did my mother have to undergo triple-bypass, valve-replacement heart surgery at such a young age? All my friends were worrying about their Friday night plans, and I was wondering if my mother was going to live. I felt so alone, as if no one in the world could understand how I was feeling.

I got up from my bed and lit the candle my mom had given me. It was a blue candle with butterflies on it, symbolic of my mother's presence in the world. Before going into surgery, my mom had told me to light it if I was missing her, and I would remember that she was there. As I sat and watched the candle burn, however, I was suddenly aware of God's presence around me. I closed my eyes and imagined I was walking on the beach, having a conversation with God. I could not see God, yet I could hear his voice around me, and I knew that he was there. I began speaking to God, asking questions. God, what if my mom dies? How could I live without her? What would happen to my family? God listened as I voiced my worries, my ultimate fear of being alone. He did not reply immediately, and I continued walking down the beach. Why aren't you answering me? I demanded. I stopped walking and looked up at the sky, wondering why God, too, had seemed to abandon me. And then I saw it, gracefully floating through the air toward me, a beautiful monarch butterfly. It flew in circles around me, as if it were trying to communicate with me. Suddenly I realized I had received my answer from God. I did not need to worry about being alone if my mother died, because she would never leave me. Even if she were to die in this very moment, I could always find her within my heart.

I watched as the butterfly floated away toward the sunset. As it disappeared I was immediately overcome with panic, that same sense of desperate loneliness I feared. But then I remembered what I needed to do; I closed my eyes and searched within my heart, and I was met with the comforting picture of my mother. I could hear her voice, her comforting words. "I love you, Lauren," I heard her say. And in that moment, I realized that everything would be okay.

Suzanne Curry
Immaculate Heart Academy
Westwood, New Jersey

Tears from Heaven

A little less than a year ago, my friend's grandmother died. My friend was very close to her grandma and often talked about her. She frequently commented on how witty, fun, and kind her grandma was. When her grandmother died, my friend lost not only a relative but a sincere and true friend.

A couple of days after her grandmother's death, my friend returned to school. She was overwhelmed with all the work she had to make up and became very upset and frustrated. She just could not concentrate on her work. How could she after she had lost such an important part of her life?

There was one day that is still clear in my mind, and that I will never forget. It was a gloomy and rainy day in April. My friend and I had geometry class last period. The class dragged on, and I noticed my friend was really struggling. Finally the bell rang, and everyone left the classroom except for the teacher, my friend, and me. I knew I had to go to softball practice, but that could wait. I had to make sure my friend was all right. She was staying after school to get extra help on the work she had missed. Not two minutes after the bell rang and before the teacher began to help her, I noticed that tears began to well up in her eyes. I knew that she wasn't upset with the fact that she didn't understand the work; something else was on her mind.

The teacher knew about my friend's grandmother, and I suggested that I take my friend for a walk, or to the bathroom—

anything that would help calm her down. So my friend and I loaded up on tissues and began to walk through the school. What happened was amazing: in every hallway we walked down, at least two people stopped to ask if my friend was all right. They could have just kept going and ignored my friend, and not be concerned with her at all. Instead, all these people took time out of their busy day, if only for just a couple of seconds, to support their classmate. This was one time when I noticed God's presence during that day.

Although it was drizzling outside, my friend and I decided to take a walk around the building. Both she and I needed a breath of fresh air. As we walked around the school, I felt the cold and bitter wind biting at my face and the cool raindrops falling on my head. Even though the weather was cold, I felt a sense of warmth and happiness run through my body. My friend continued to express the emotions she had been feeling lately: anger, fear, sadness, and frustration. At the end of our little "journey" around the school, however, we began to walk in silence. It began to rain a little harder, and I watched the rain-drops fall from the sky. Then I looked at my friend. She still had tears in her eyes, but she was also mesmerized by the natural mystery of the rain. We continued walking.

When we got back inside, my friend looked up at me with a smile. This was the first time she had smiled in days. She looked at me and thanked me for taking time out of my day to help her in a time of need. I told her that she was the one to be thanked, for she gave me the gift of friendship and led me through the rain and into the doorway where I could see and experience God.

The Whole World Was Crying

Therese
Mount Saint Charles
Academy
Woonsocket, Rhode Island

"Erin is dead." My mind went blank. My eleven-year-old ears were hearing these words, but my eleven-year-old mind was having a hard time comprehending them. A million questions raced through my thoughts: How? When? Where? Why? That last question is the only one I did not speak, and I knew there was no answer. No one could explain to me why Erin had died, but the truth was she was gone. I would have to accept that. I would have to accept that death can take someone anytime it wants, even on a Friday morning in March. Even harder, I would have to accept that death can take anyone it wants, even a twenty-four-year-old newlywed a week before her birthday.

When I first look back, that weekend is one long, confusing mess, and everything blurs together. When I really stop and think about it though, image after image comes to my mind. One detail really sticks out: a dress, peach-colored and flowered. I loathed it, but Erin loved it. I wore it to her wake.

The wake was one long endless afternoon, overflowing with people and flowers. Everywhere I turned there were tears and hugs and well-meaning people saying things like, "Don't worry, Erin's in a better place now." I spent the time in a small room with my brother and sister. None of us went in to see her, even though a part of me desperately wanted to. It's not that I was scared, but it was just too strange. As the afternoon went on, I got more and more curious. I would try to sneak glimpses of Erin from outside the room. Something though, maybe a wall, was always in my way. I gave up.

Before long we were on our way home. In the car I felt the need to ask my mom questions about the smallest details. "What was Erin wearing?" "Were there lots of people?" "Did our flowers look nice?" "Was anybody crying?" I think in some way I needed the answers to these questions. A part of me still could not believe my aunt had died, and these answers would validate for me that Erin was, in fact, dead.

Any doubts I may have had were erased the next day, at the funeral. Erin was being laid to rest on a cloudy and overcast Tuesday morning, three days before her birthday. As I stood in the back of the church, waiting to follow Erin's casket into her final Mass, I remember thinking how unfair it was. Erin had planned better than this. Now that she was married, someday she was going to have a little girl. She was always saying that she wanted a little girl just like my sister and me. But that was not to be for Erin. I was reminded of this with every step I took behind her casket. Erin's dead, Erin's dead, Erin's dead echoed through my head all the way down the aisle. Finally after what seemed like years, we reached the front pew. I settled down into my seat, but I couldn't pay attention to the Mass. Instead I studied every corner of the church, I took in everything. To the left of me was Erin's casket, draped in white cloth. To the right of me was my uncle, burying his wife of three months. And behind me, everywhere I turned, were Erin's relatives, people weeping for whatever Erin was to them: a sister, a daughter, a niece, a cousin. This was the moment it was seared into my mind: that the impossible was possible, and Erin Marie Driscoll was dead. Really and truly dead and gone and about to be buried, because by now her funeral Mass had ended. I got up and followed her casket the way it had come in, knowing this would be the last time I would ever be in the presence of Erin. And as I stood on the steps and watched Erin's casket being loaded into the hearse for her final ride, it began to rain. I looked up to the heavens and then to the rain, and it seemed like the whole world was crying.

Sean Nugent
Saint John the Baptist
Diocesan High School
West Islip, New York

Doubting, Trusting, and Mimi

There have been times, though not many, when I have asked God, "Why?" One time that really sticks out in my mind has to do with something that happened to my grandma, Mimi. You have to really know her to understand the situation. Mimi is the best grandma a kid could have. She was eighty-one years old at the time. She couldn't see too well, but that never stopped her. She would drive to church every morning for Mass and she'd do just about anything for me and my brothers.

About four years ago, Mimi was on her way to the store to buy Halloween candy for the trick-or-treaters. On her way to the car, she fell in her driveway and hit her eye on the pavement. She lives alone, so it was lucky the gardeners were there—otherwise I don't think she would be alive today. The gardeners rushed Mimi to the hospital. Her eye had been shattered from the fall, and the doctors tried to repair it but couldn't. She was in the hospital for a very long time and had two operations. In the second operation, they removed the eye. I was in fifth grade when all this was going on, and I started to question God. I would say things like, "Are you really there, God?" and "God, why do such bad things happen to such good people?" As other bad things happened in my life, I continued questioning God and the existence of God.

Mimi recuperated as best she could. She lived with us for a few months until she got her strength back. Then she decided to go to California for the winter and stay with my Aunt Peggy. Well, that was the year of the big earthquake in Los Angeles. The epicenter was five miles from my aunt's house, and Mimi was thrown out of bed and hit on the head by a lamp. She was back at our house in three days and stayed with us for a few more months.

Mimi will be eighty-six in a few weeks. Since she has gotten better, it has drastically changed my view of faith. When Mimi was hurt, I did not have much faith in God. But when she got better, I began to trust God more and more. Mimi never lost her faith or questioned God, and that taught me a lesson. She still thanked God that she had one eye.

It seems that when good things happen in my life, I trust God a lot more. Now I have learned that even though God allows good and bad things to happen, you should not lose your faith in God.

Right now in my faith life, I believe in the existence of God, and I have lots of faith in him. When bad things happen, I almost never question or doubt God. Even though people occasionally ask, "Why, God?" I say "Thank God!" An old Irish saying sums it up for me: "When you wake up in the morning, get on your knees and thank God that you're on your feet."

Audrey M. Ruzicka
Saint Elizabeth Academy
Saint Louis, Missouri

God Made Everything Perfect

As I sit here thinking back on my life, I realize that I have had a good one. When I needed God, he was always there. A time I really felt God's presence was when my need lasted for about six months.

It all started like this: In July my mom was diagnosed with cancer, first in the spine and then in other parts, like the lungs and the brain. The day she found out was my sixteenth birthday. When she told me, we just sat and cried together for about an hour. We decided we needed to tell my brother and sister, so I sat there holding her hand while she talked on the phone. Eventually we told the whole family. And we decided that day that we were going to see the beach again. The next day we planned a trip. Everyone went, and I mean everyone: Grandma, Grandpa, aunts, uncles, and cousins. August twelfth we were on our way. We all had a wonderful time. It was like God made everything perfect! We were all sorry when we had to go back home.

As time went on, my mom got sicker every day. But we didn't let it bother us. We still played gin rummy and talked. We treated every day that she had left as special. We talked about what was happening to her and how she would get better. She never did. Well, time passed rather quickly, and she kept getting sicker and sicker. In November we had several special days, like my parents twenty-fourth wedding anniversary, Thanksgiving, and Christmas—that's right, Christmas! It was a little early, but it felt like Christmas! One Saturday in November, when everyone was home and she was feeling pretty good, we all decided to put up the Christmas decorations. Later that day we had our friends over to a big dinner. Everything was so perfect, God must have blessed us again. Mom said that it was the best day of her life, and I believed her! Around that time I went on retreat for three days, and when I got home, she looked really bad.

I thought, "How could God do this? What did she do to God?" I got very angry with God, but that is when he told me I could get by. I don't know how to explain it—I just felt it. Around the sixth of December, my mom started to talk uncontrollably, kind of like she was reliving her life. She couldn't stop smiling. She said some really funny things! Well, we listened to her for about two days. On the next day, in the evening, my grandparents and some of my aunts and uncles came over. We prayed around her all evening, till everyone decided they needed some sleep and went home. Around then she looked straight at me, and I *know* she knew it was me, and gave me the biggest and best hug in the world. I sat there for about an hour rubbing her head (I made a nickel). She became really calm and fell asleep, so I went to bed. At 3:00 a.m. my dad woke me up and told me to come downstairs. She had died, but we weren't really sure—we hoped she was just in a coma. We all sat around her for about an hour before we called anyone. We sat there and joked and laughed like she wouldn't let us cry (eventually I did plenty of that).

The next three days, I felt like I was living in a dream and couldn't wake up. That is when my friends showed me how much they really cared. They did so much for us. I know God must have been with me during those months, because the good times we shared were *so* good, and going through this experience wasn't as bad as I thought it was going to be.

Olivia Zehner
Bishop Grimes High
School
East Syracuse, New York

Finding
My Road

There are many ways in which people experience the presence of God in their lives: some through the miracle of forgiveness, some through traumatic experiences in their lives, and some through the works of other people.

When we are young, we are asked many times what we want to be when we grow up. All my life I have been asked this same question. I have been encouraged to become an artist, a dancer, a writer, and even a lawyer. I have thought a lot about these suggestions. I've always been taught that you could be whatever you want, but just to be sure you do what makes you happy and you will be successful. Yes, it would be fun to be a dancer, an artist, or a lawyer, yet I could never think of something I really wanted to do, something I knew I could live for, something that fit my purpose in life. The only thing I knew was that I was here for a reason, and in some way or another, I would make a difference.

God seems to do much of his work in small, seemingly trivial experiences that can profoundly change a person's life—

I went on a school trip to Washington, D.C., the capitol of the homeless. As I walked the streets with my friends, visiting all the important monuments, I could not help but focus on the not-so-glorious part of D.C. I was amazed at the number of homeless people wandering the streets, some begging, some just resting. All weekend long, all I could focus on was the plight of those people. It became depressing.

On the last day, a Sunday morning, I was on my way to get something to eat, and I came across a young, black, homeless man. He approached me and the group I was with, and he began to entertain us with his unique ability to rap. Most of my friends kept going, but my friend Brad and I decided to stay and listen to the man. His talent amazed me. When he was through, we applauded, and he asked us for money. I thought about this for a second and then asked him if a hot lunch would interest him more. I took the last bit of my spending money and bought the man a hot dog with everything on it, a bag of chips, and a soda. The man was so grateful, and as he walked away, he said, "Thank you, and God bless you."

And God did bless me. My heart was so overwhelmed with happiness and love—it could only have been that God was present. I realized then that for me, helping others in need was how the love of God was revealed in my heart. I realized it was something I could do and be happy with for the rest of my life. This experience did not tell me exactly what I want to do "when I grow up," but it did show me the road I eventually will travel.

Becky Crone
Saint Agnes Academy
Memphis, Tennessee

Mandy Tahlmore
Morris Catholic
High School
Denville, New Jersey

In the Living and the Dying

The presence of God was never less visible to me than when my grandpa was sick. I raised many questions with my family and friends. I got answers like "God always has a reason" and "God knows what he is doing" and even "Grandpa will soon be at peace forever." They were all good answers, for someone five years younger, but not for a teenager like myself. Many teens doubt the presence of God. Even I did!

The day my grandpa died was filled with confusion, yet it changed my life forever. I went to my grandma's house to take care of my cousins. My four-year-old cousin came up to me and asked, "Why did Grandpa leave?" At first all I could think was that it was a very good question! Why *did* he leave? I took a good look in my little cousin's eyes and said: "I don't know. Only God knows what's best for Grandpa, and even though he seems far away, he's not. You can still talk to him whenever you want. God's angels are watching over Grandpa, and he is watching over you and me with a big smile, because he loves us." I finally had the answer to the question I had been asking everyone else.

As I watched my grandpa's twelve wonderful children and forty grandchildren all pitch in to help, I thought to myself, What a family! Everyone was going out of their way to make my grandma comfortable. Even if the size of paper cups didn't please her, no one argued. They ran out and bought the right size. Preparing for the wake and the funeral was very hard. All the adults sat around the kitchen table and very delicately helped Grandma cope with the preparations.

The viewing was very hard to grasp. I could never have imagined my grandpa so lifeless. I was used to seeing him joking with the nurses and playing with the grandchildren. He used to bring the older cousins out for root beer and hot dogs. Or he would be beating one of us at a game of chess or pinochle. Every single one of us has caught him in front of one of his John Wayne westerns. He never missed those. He even had a "John Wayne room," where he displayed his Conestoga wagons and his horse-and-buggy models and the bold posters of John Wayne with that gentle smile. Most important, Grandpa displayed his big, fluffy teddy bears. These stuffed animals were most like my grandpa. He had the gentle teddy-bear smile that *everyone* loved. It was irreplaceable!

The funeral was beautiful. The priest said it was the most beautiful service he had ever taken part in. He called it "a time of retreat." He said that he had never seen a family come together and be such an example of God's family as we were that day. Those words keep me at peace with God.

Three months later we had a "surprise birthday party" for my grandpa. We all sat around telling stories, laughing about the good times and shedding a few tears about the sadder memories. We quietly contemplated all the times we had spent together as a family. That night the whole family squeezed in for a picture. My cousin's friend Michelle was there, and she took the picture. As squashed as we were, we couldn't have been more comfortable!

The next day I realized something. Michelle had witnessed the most awe-inspiring gift, one that some people never get to experience—the gift of love. I look at our family and see the togetherness that we feel. Most people would be jealous at the sight of it. It was so magnificent that I cannot explain it! Every day I talk to my grandpa and tell him what a wonderful family he helped bring together. I see the presence of God in my family, and dearly give thanks for that. My grandpa taught me all about life, both in his living and in his dying.

David Luth
Peninsula Catholic
High School
Newport News, Virginia

God Is Good

One day when I was on vacation, I felt the presence of God. My whole family was in the van (six people including me). I was driving. There was also a lot of stuff in the van, and we were all very squashed. We were on our way to Moberly, Missouri, to see my cousin Andrea get married. My dad made the decision that we would only stop for bathroom breaks and short rests until we got to my grandmother's house near Saint Louis. Starting from Virginia, that's nineteen hours in the car.

We had all gotten up at 4:00 a.m. and were on the road by 5:00. We were all extremely tired and grumpy. We were happy to be going on vacation, but were not looking forward to the cramped space of the van. It was the middle of summer, too, so it was extremely hot. The body heat of six people does not help to cool the car, especially when the air conditioner is broken.

More than six hours into the trip, close to noon, we all had been awake for some time. I was especially hot and sweaty, and I got into a quarrel with my older sisters about some petty thing. I don't even remember what it was about. I was about to blow up at them, but for some reason I decided to hold it in, which was very difficult.

We were driving through West Virginia and were in the mountains. The constant winding of the road was making me sick, and I was getting grumpy again. As I was driving, I saw down below a valley surrounded by mountains. I saw little tiny houses and roads and cars—they all seemed to have been miniaturized. Clouds drifted by at eye level in between the mountaintops, and the sun shone down on the valley. You could see huge shadows made by the clouds. What made the sight even more spectacular was that the mountains were completely covered in green by all different kinds of trees. It was one of the most beautiful sights I had ever seen.

I completely forgot about the quarrel and started thinking about how great God was to make something so beautiful, how much God loved me to make that valley. The sight calmed me, and I felt his presence.

Liz Bertko
Bishop O'Dowd High
School
Oakland, California

Encountering God

I have seen the face of God. Broad, stern jaw, thick brows, deep eyes. Dimples. Sometimes I see a tree trunk, tall and sturdy; sometimes a dancer, waiflike and graceful, swaying in the breeze. The face of God.

Sometimes God is a tearful child, trying to hide underneath a blanket of sorrow; or a warrior, strong and passionate; or the old man who walks his dog in front of my house every morning, struggling to make it up the hill each day. Sometimes God is sunshine, beating upon my back on a hot summer's day; or a stroke of moonlight reflecting on the water, cut into a thousand glittering pieces. Or merely a flicker of existence

I can see God watching us, eyes intent, compassionate, sorrowful. God has eyes filled with laughter, with pride, with pain, with pleasure. God has the eyes of a frightened doe at that final moment of truth, with the headlights lighting up features and the growling of a car engine growing closer and closer. . . .

I have seen God's footsteps: in the mud, in the sky, on the first day after the rain has stopped. I have seen God's footsteps: after the Great Fire, when the earth and sky were bleeding and mourning, the hills and trees blackened and dead, the sun in the sky still flushed with anger.

It was then that I stood over a blackened abyss, questioning, staring, shivering. I had not realized that the darkness was so cold. And I hid in that darkness for a time, not a sad darkness nor a frightened one but one without emotion, cut off from the rest of the world. It was a silent darkness, without a sign of pain or passion or glory. I shouted, *"Why?"* into this unbearable abyss, and it did not echo onto a cliff nearby but was consumed . . . my passion swallowed up whole. This was Doubt, the masked fiend, eating away at me, chewing my heart and body and soul into nothingness.

For a time Doubt persisted, eating up my mind, causing me to question if God had heard me or if he really was there at all. But my answer came eventually . . . with the flowers of spring. Flowers yellow and red and purple that covered the black abyss and turned nothingness into hope. Daffodils, sour grass, lupine. And I knew that God had answered. I had heard the voice of God.

Index by School

Duchesne High School
Saint Charles, MO
Brad Amiri   33

Father Judge High School
Philadelphia, PA
Brian Weber   78

Immaculate Heart Academy
Westwood, NJ
Suzanne Curry   114
Allison Hodges   26
Lauren Zwicky   111

John F. Kennedy Memorial High School
Burien, WA
J. A. M.   89

Kennedy–Kenrick Catholic High School
Norristown, PA
Christopher Beaver   24
Megan Jefferies   81
Joseph J. Omlor   17

Lake Michigan Catholic High School
Saint Joseph, MI
Charlie Binger   41
Amber Rodriguez   62
Laura Kay Slavicek   35

Morris Catholic High School
Denville, NJ
Mandy Tahlmore   125

Mount Notre Dame High School
Cincinnati, OH
Erin Keegan   83
Ashley Wiese   64

Mount Saint Charles Academy
Woonsocket, RI
Jaymee Marois   57
Manpreet Sidhu   108
Therese   116

Notre Dame Academy
Toledo, OH
Jessica Carnicom   cover

Our Lady of Good Counsel High School
Wheaton, MD
Rebecca Bishop   40

Peninsula Catholic High School
Newport News, VA
Adam Law   87
David Luth   127

Saint Agnes Academic School
College Point, NY
Providence G. Curatolo   28

Saint Agnes Academy
Memphis, TN
Becky Crone   124
Megan Smith   16
Maria Tilly   103

Saint Aloysius High School
Vicksburg, MS
Casey Franco   70

Saint Barnabas High School
Bronx, NY
K. B.   46

Saint Charles Catholic High School
LaPlace, LA
B. B. 92

Saint Elizabeth Academy
Saint Louis, MO
Alison Rusan-Long 51
Audrey M. Ruzicka 120
Angela Elaine Maria Yust 74

Saint Gertrude High School
Richmond, VA
Lindsay Clampitt 66

Saint John the Baptist Diocesan High School
West Islip, NY
Danny Brosnahan 49
Sean Nugent 118

Saint Mark's High School
Wilmington, DE
Michaela 97

Saint Xavier High School
Louisville, KY
Mike McGlothlen 96

Santa Clara High School
Oxnard, CA
Becky Bennett 22

Stella Maris High School
Rockaway, NY
Michelle Schaeffer 106

Trinity High School
Garfield, OH
Veronica Molina 32

Villa Maria Academy
Malvern, PA
Katie Luzi 13